D0461070

How to Use This Book

Look for these special features in this book:

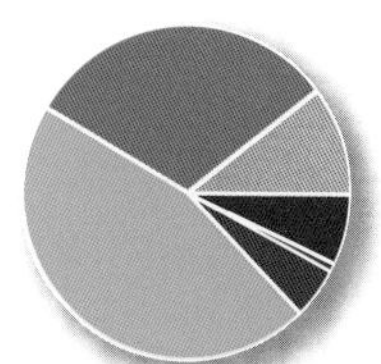

SIDEBARS, **CHARTS**, **GRAPHS**, and original **MAPS** expand your understanding of what's being discussed—and also make useful sources for classroom reports.

FAQs answer common **F**requently **A**sked **Q**uestions about people, places, and things.

WOW FACTORS offer "Who knew?" facts to keep you thinking.

TRAVEL GUIDE gives you tips on exploring the state—either in person or right from your chair!

PROJECT ROOM provides fun ideas for school assignments and incredible research projects. Plus, there's a guide to primary sources—what they are and how to cite them.

Please note: All statistics are as up-to-date as possible at the time of publication. Population data is taken from the 2010 census.

Consultants: Debra B. Faulkner, History Instructor, Metropolitan State College of Denver; Stephen Leonard, History Department Chair, Metropolitan State College of Denver; William Loren Katz; Jerry Magloughlin, Department of Geosciences, Colorado State University

Book production by The Design Lab

Library of Congress Cataloging-in-Publication Data
Somervill, Barbara A.
Colorado / by Barbara A. Somervill. — Revised edition.
pages cm. — (America the beautiful. Third series)
Includes bibliographical references and index.
ISBN 978-0-531-24878-2 (lib. bdg.)
1. Colorado—Juvenile literature. I. Title.
F776.3.S67 2014
978.8—dc23 2013031192

Printed in the United States of America 141

1 2 3 4 5 6 7 8 9 10 R 23 22 21 20 19 18 17 16 15 14

Colorado

BY BARBARA A. SOMERVILL

Third Series, Revised Edition

Children's Press®
An Imprint of Scholastic Inc.
New York ★ Toronto ★ London ★ Auckland ★ Sydney
Mexico City ★ New Delhi ★ Hong Kong
Danbury, Connecticut

CONTENTS

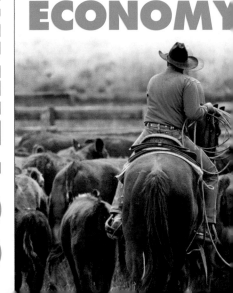

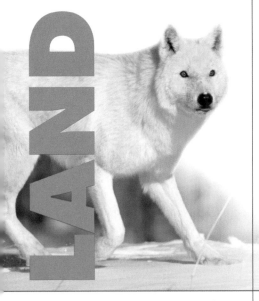

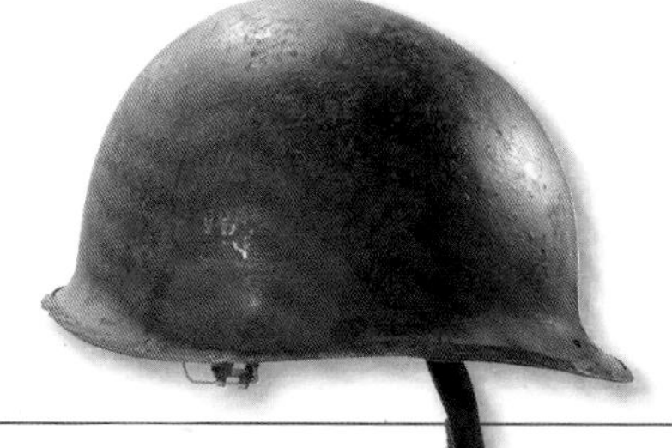

PROJECT ROOM

★

QUICK FACTS

State capital: Denver
Largest city: Denver
Total area: 104,094 square miles (269,603 sq km)
Highest point: Mount Elbert, 14,440 feet (4,401 m)
Lowest point: Arikaree River, 3,315 feet (1,010 m)

WYOMING

NEBRASKA

UTAH

Rocky Mountain National Park

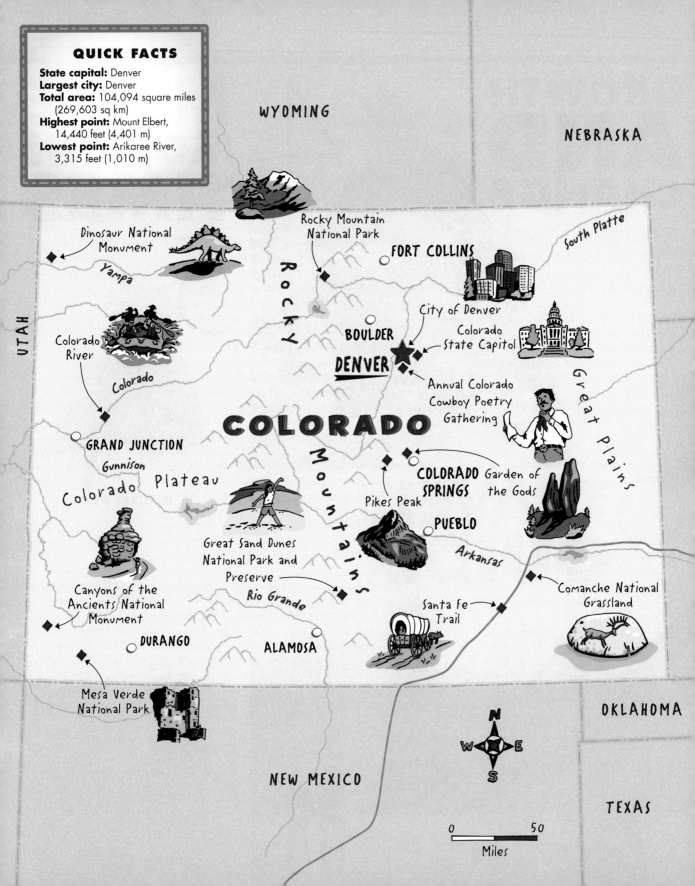

Dinosaur National Monument

FORT COLLINS

South Platte

Yampa

Rocky Mountains

BOULDER

City of Denver

Colorado State Capitol

Colorado River

DENVER

Colorado

Annual Colorado Cowboy Poetry Gathering

COLORADO

Great Plains

GRAND JUNCTION

Gunnison

Colorado Plateau

COLORADO SPRINGS

Garden of the Gods

Pikes Peak

PUEBLO

Great Sand Dunes National Park and Preserve

Arkansas

Canyons of the Ancients National Monument

Rio Grande

Santa Fe Trail

Comanche National Grassland

DURANGO

ALAMOSA

Mesa Verde National Park

OKLAHOMA

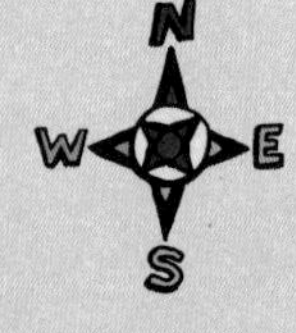

NEW MEXICO

TEXAS

0 50
Miles

Welcome to Colorado!

HOW DID COLORADO GET ITS NAME?

Colorado got its name from the red mud in its rushing river water. Spanish explorer Francisco Vásquez de Coronado and his men began exploring the Southwest in 1540. His troops called the river they saw *colorado*, which is Spanish for "ruddy" or "reddish." In the west, the Colorado River cuts through dark red canyons. Jutting rocks burn a deep russet red in the sunlight at Garden of the Gods Park. Red ribbons of sediment line the cliffs surrounding the trails of Glenwood Canyon. Everywhere you turn in Colorado, you'll see red in all its hues.

READ ABOUT

The Maroon Bells peaks in the autumn

LAND

★

WHEN MOST PEOPLE HEAR "COLORADO," THEY THINK SNOWCAPPED MOUNTAINS AND RUGGED LANDSCAPES. That mental picture is accurate—five different mountain ranges rise in Colorado. The highest peak, Mount Elbert, stands 14,440 feet (4,401 meters) above sea level. At 3,315 feet (1,010 m) above sea level, even Colorado's lowest point, where the Arikaree River flows from Colorado into Kansas, is higher than some other states' highest points. Mountains, rivers, high desert, and sweeping plains combine to make Colorado the eighth-largest state, with a total area of 104,094 square miles (269,603 square kilometers).

Ranches are common on the fertile land of the San Juan mountain range.

MOUNTAIN BUILDING

More than 300 million years ago, Colorado's plants and animals lived in a mix of desert and tropical climates—warm breezes and mild winters. Then two landmasses collided along a geological fault. Their slow, forceful meeting poked the earliest Rocky Mountains, called the Ancestral Rockies, up into the landscape. Those earliest mountains eroded over the next tens of millions of years, leaving behind several now well-known beds of red rock.

By 200 million years ago, the Colorado region must have become a dinosaur's paradise, because scientists have discovered hundreds of fossil remains from dinosaurs along the Colorado-Utah border.

Between 170 million and 40 million years ago, three more collisions between some of Earth's landmasses built more mountains in western North America. The last episode, called the Laramide Orogeny, which began around 75 million years ago, gave us the Rocky Mountains—high, rugged peaks and deep, plunging valleys.

LAND REGIONS

Colorado lies in the southwestern quarter of the United States. Nearly rectangular in shape, it borders seven other states. Going clockwise, with Colorado in the center of the dial, Wyoming is at 12 o'clock, Nebraska at 2, Kansas at 3, Oklahoma at 4, New Mexico at 6, Arizona at 8, and Utah at 9.

The Rocky Mountains occupy the central third of the state. To the far west lie the Colorado Plateau and a small section called the Intermontane Basin. To the east lies a high plains region of the Great Plains that takes up another 40 percent of the land.

Colorado Topography

Use the color-coded elevation chart to see on the map Colorado's high points (dark red to orange) and low points (green to dark green). Elevation is measured as the distance above or below sea level.

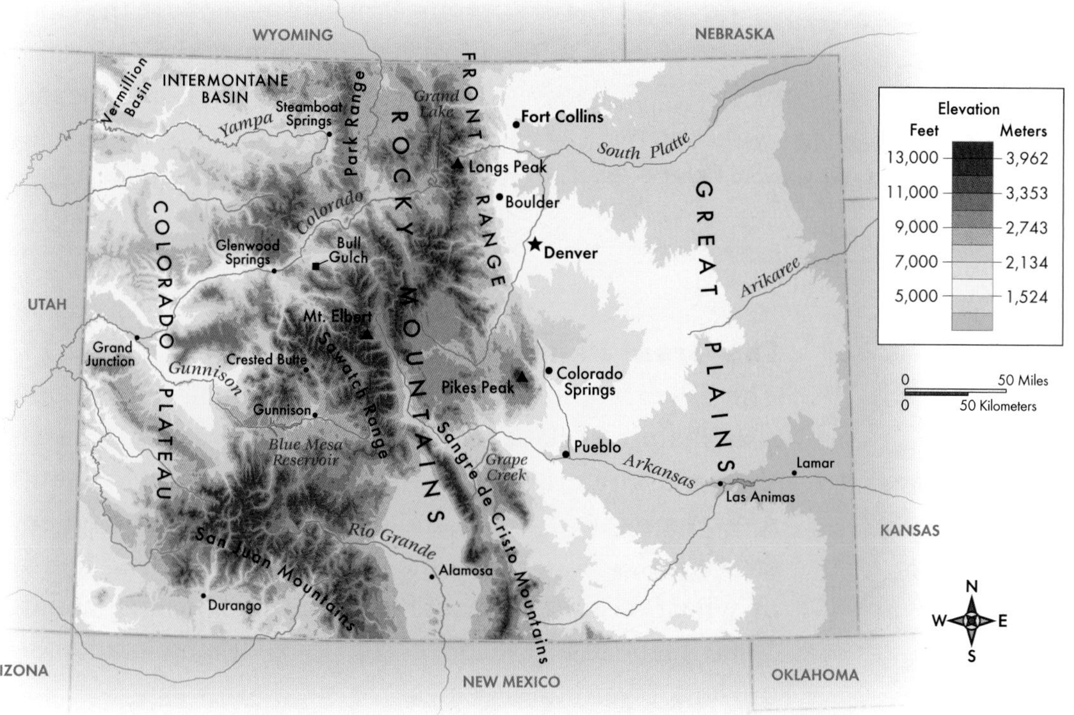

MINI-BIO

ZEBULON PIKE: EXPLORER

Zebulon Pike (1779–1813) grew up in Lamberton, New Jersey, now part of Trenton. At age 20, he became a commissioned officer in the military. An 1806 expedition took Pike and his men into Colorado to explore land gained in the Louisiana Purchase. Pike saw the peak that now bears his name, but he did not climb it. He had a poor opinion of the land, stating that the region was not useful for farming. He did say, "Of all countries ever visited by the footsteps of civilized man, there never was one probably that produced game in greater abundance." During the War of 1812 (1812–1814), he commanded troops at the Battle of York and was killed.

Want to know more? Visit www.factsfornow.scholastic.com and enter the keyword **Colorado.**

Rocky Mountain Region

The Rocky Mountain region in Colorado is actually several different mountain ranges. They include the Front Range, the Park Range, the Sawatch, the San Juans, and the Sangre de Cristo mountains. The average elevation in the state is 6,800 feet (2,073 m) above sea level, higher than any other state.

Mesas are flat-topped mountains; buttes are hills that jut out from the land and are also flat-topped. The Colorado Plateau, west of the Rockies, is an eerie land of mesas, buttes, deep valleys, and strange rock formations. In the land of mesas and buttes, the Colorado River cuts a deep path as it heads toward the Pacific Ocean. In the northwest, the Intermontane Basin is a region of rolling forested hills, dotted with sagebrush.

WOW

Every year, 400,000 people ascend Pikes Peak, 14,115 feet (4,302 m) above sea level. Katharine Lee Bates wrote the words to "America the Beautiful" after visiting the mountain by wagon in 1893.

The Great Plains

The eastern land, a small part of the Great Plains, consists mainly of flatlands with some rolling hills. This is short-grass prairie land, where wild grasses once sent roots deep into the soil, and bison and deer browsed on the shoots. Today, it is home to farms with endless fields of wheat, corn, or hay. This is the high plains, about 3,000 feet (914 m) above sea level, rising gradually upward toward the Rockies.

RIVERS AND LAKES

Some 20 rivers (six major ones) have their **headwaters** in the Colorado Rockies. Most continents have at least one elevated location that determines the direction in which waters flow. In North America's Rocky Mountains it is called the Continental Divide. Rivers on the eastern side flow toward the Atlantic Ocean; on the western side, they flow toward the Pacific.

On the western side, the Colorado River rushes toward the Pacific Ocean. The Colorado begins its 1,450-mile (2,330 km) journey in the Rockies and ends in the Gulf of California in Mexico. Along its route, it drains runoff water from Utah, New Mexico, Arizona, Nevada, and California. From the eastern slopes of the Rockies, the Rio Grande, Arkansas, South Platte, North Platte, and Republican rivers flow toward the Atlantic. Along with the Colorado, these river basins form the primary **watersheds** of Colorado.

WORDS TO KNOW

headwaters *the streams that make up the beginnings of a river*

watersheds *land areas that drain water from a particular region*

Colorado Geo-Facts

Along with the state's geographical highlights, this chart ranks Colorado's land, water, and total area compared to all other states.

Total area; rank	104,094 square miles (269,603 sq km); 8th
Land; rank	103,718 square miles (268,630 sq km); 8th
Water; rank	376 square miles (974 sq km); 46th
Inland water; rank	376 square miles (974 sq km); 40th
Geographic center	Park County, 30 miles (48 km) northwest of Pikes Peak
Latitude	37° N to 41° N
Longitude	102° W to 109° W
Highest point	Mount Elbert, 14,440 feet (4,401 m)
Lowest point	Arikaree River, 3,315 feet (1,010 m)
Largest city	Denver
Longest river	Colorado

Source: U.S. Census Bureau, 2010 census

Colorado is slightly smaller than Nevada, and more than 67 times the size of Rhode Island. In international terms, it is slightly larger than New Zealand.

Boaters navigate the waters of the Colorado River.

Colorado has more than 500 lakes, and most are found in the mountains. Grand Lake is Colorado's largest natural lake, situated in Rocky Mountain National Park. Some other major bodies of water were formed when dams were built to control the flow of Colorado's rivers. The 20-mile (32 km) long Blue Mesa Reservoir, on the Gunnison River, is actually the state's largest body of water, complete with its own salmon fishery. Many of Colorado's small lakes provide excellent boating and fishing. Most Colorado lakes are snow fed, which makes them too cold for swimming.

For a more comfortable dip, Colorado has more than 93 hot springs, many of which are open for public bathing. Their waters can range from bathtub warm to scalding hot. The most popular are mineral springs where, for a fee, visitors can soak away aches and pains. Colorado's Native Americans have bathed in these delightful hot springs for centuries. Among the largest are those in Glenwood Springs and Pagosa Springs.

CLIMATE

Colorado's climate is known as highland continental, which means cold, dry winters and relatively warm summers. It is hard to think that a place that gets so much snow is dry, but only the western slopes of the Rockies accumulate much snow. Grand Junction in the west and Denver in the east get little snow compared to mountain towns such as Steamboat Springs and Crested Butte.

Because of Colorado's varied terrain, temperatures can differ greatly from one place to another. Over the 90-mile (145 km) stretch between Pikes Peak and Las Animas, temperatures can be 35 degrees Fahrenheit (19 degrees Celsius) different. That is the same temperature spread as found on average between Miami, Florida, and Reykjavík, Iceland, each year!

SNOWFALL AMOUNTS

Location	Average Annual Snowfall in inches (centimeters)
Denver	57.5″ (146 cm)
Steamboat Springs	171″ (434 cm)
Grand Junction	22″ (56 cm)
Crested Butte	215.8″ (548 cm)
Colorado Springs	44.6″ (113 cm)

An avalanche in the San Juan mountains

In areas where large amounts of snow accumulate, there is danger of avalanches. Avalanches most often occur on steep slopes. A loud noise, sudden movement, or even wind gusts can trigger an avalanche. The snow roars down the mountainside, reaching speeds of up to 30 miles per hour (48 kilometers per hour). The state experiences more than 2,000 avalanches yearly, and some prove deadly.

WOW

During the winter of 1978–1979, Wolf Creek Pass, in southwestern Colorado, was blanketed by nearly 70 feet (21 m) of snow—about the height of a seven-story building.

Blizzards are always a danger in parts of Colorado. In December 2006, two blizzards swept across the state, creating 80-inch (203 centimeter) snowdrifts in some Denver locations and closing down airports and major highways. In a blizzard, people may become stranded, accidents occur, and there is a danger of death or illness from hypothermia, a condition that occurs when a body is too cold for too long. A blizzard often reduces visibility, making driving, walking, or any other mode of transportation difficult. After the snow stops, cleanup becomes an around-the-clock job.

Spring in Colorado is blustery and changeable. There is as likely to be a late-season blizzard as there is a warm sunny day, and weather changes can be quick and dramatic.

Summers are hotter on the high plains, with temperatures occasionally reaching over 100 °F (38 °C). People on the plains experience startling thunderstorms with rumbling thunderclaps and brilliant flashes of lightning.

Cooler days and nights at higher elevations make mountain living more comfortable than the plains in summer. A typical mountain day would see a high in the 80 °F (27 °C) range, and night would be about 20 °F (11 °C) cooler.

Occasionally, summer in Colorado is very hot. This heat, paired with the low humidity common throughout the state, can lead to forest and grassland fires. Lightning strikes and careless humans start about 2,500 forest fires yearly in Colorado. Most are controllable, but some spread quickly and dangerously. The state's most destructive fire took place in 2013 near Colorado Springs in Black Forest. The wildfire destroyed nearly 500 homes and killed two people.

Weather Report

This chart shows record temperatures (high and low) for the state, as well as average temperatures (July and January) and average annual precipitation.

Record high temperature . . . 114°F (46°C) at Las Animas on July 1, 1933, and at Sedgewick on July 11, 1954

Record low temperature . . . . –61°F (–52°C) at Maybell in Moffat County on February 1, 1985

Average July temperature, Burlington . . . . 74°F (23°C)

Average July temperature, Leadville . . . . 55°F (13°C)

Average January temperature, Burlington . . . . 28°F (–2°C)

Average January temperature, Leadville . . . . 18°F (–8°C)

Average annual precipitation, state . . . . 15 inches (38.1 cm)

Source: National Climatic Data Center, NESDIS, NOAA, U.S. Department of Commerce

Colorado National Park Areas

This map shows some of Colorado's national parks, monuments, preserves, and other areas protected by the National Park Service.

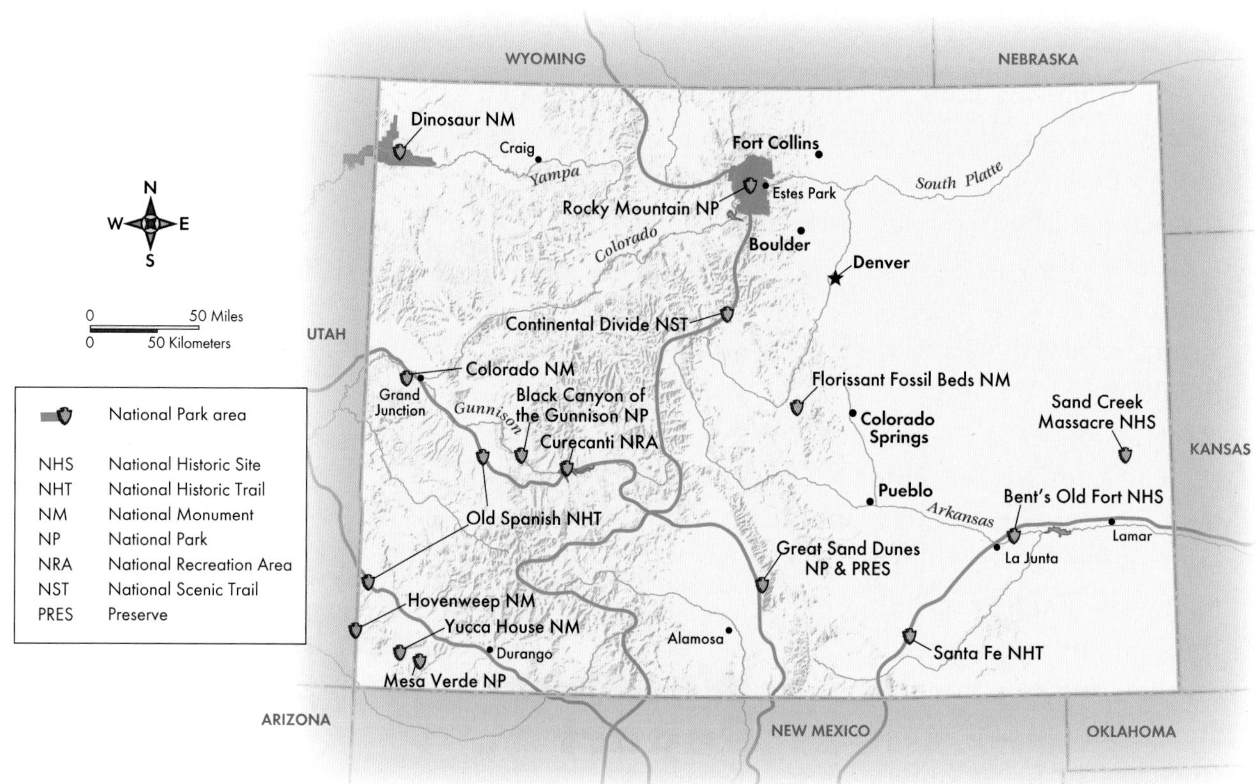

PLANT LIFE

From high plains to mountains to mesas, Colorado plant life changes dramatically. The plains are grasslands where once galleta and Indian rice grass grew in swaths among blue grama and buffalo grass. Many of the grasses in these high plains are now short grasses, rarely reaching above 2 feet (61 cm) on the surface, but with deep, complex root systems that allow them to survive fire,

Tundra sunflowers brighten the landscape in the Rocky Mountains.

HAZEL SCHMOLL: PRESERVING THE COLUMBINE

Hazel Schmoll (1890–1990) collected, recorded, and exhibited 10,000 samples of Colorado wildflowers and plants during her long career as a botanist (someone who studies plants). Raised near a mining camp in the Colorado Rockies, she spent her early years roaming the mountains on foot and horseback. While serving as state botanist, Schmoll organized a survey of the state's plant life. Late in life, she helped get the blue columbine (above) named Colorado's state flower. Another Colorado wildflower, the Schmoll milkvetch, is named for her.

Want to know more? Visit www.factsfornow.scholastic.com and enter the keyword **Colorado.**

drought, and wind. Indian paintbrush, larkspur, and pasqueflower dot the landscape that was once home to millions of bison, pronghorn, and deer.

Higher in the mountains, grasses give way to pines, spruce, birch, aspen, and alder trees. Higher still, piñon pines and juniper grow among mountain columbines, lupines, and the oddly named sneezeweed. The mountain peaks are alpine tundra, an area of mostly rock or thin soil where harsh weather prevents the growth of trees. Tundra sunflowers brighten the landscape, but

SEE IT HERE!

ALPINE TUNDRA COMMUNITIES TRAIL

Right beneath the tree line, the place in a mountain range above which trees do not normally grow, cold weather and strong winds have twisted and bent the trees so that they look like sculptures. You can see these gnarled, stunted trees, called krummholz, by taking a walk on the Alpine Tundra Communities Trail in Rocky Mountain National Park.

Colorado's oldest tree is a bristlecone pine that lives near South Park. It is about 2,455 years old!

the dominant plant life on the tundra is lichen, a plant that is a mix of fungi and algae. More than 450 types of lichen grow in Colorado's tundra regions.

Colorado's mesas are covered with pines, sagebrush, and varieties of cactus. Prickly pear cactus has been providing humans with food, drink, and medicine since hunter-gatherers roamed the high desert some 10,000 years ago.

QUAKING ASPEN

On the Colorado Plateau, a stand of quaking aspen, or aspen for short, rises 60 feet (18 m) high. In autumn, yellow aspen leaves quiver in the breeze. Aspens seem to all look alike, and that's no surprise. The trees spread by cloning. A mature aspen root system can send up to one million shoots per acre.

Aspen trunks are slender, and the bark on older trees may be covered with brown lichen. The trees' leaves are round, measuring from 1 to 2.75 inches (2.5 to 7 cm) across, with jagged edges. Aspen leaf stalks are flat and flexible, allowing the leaves to "quake" in light breezes. The branching pattern of aspens is unusual and is best seen in winter when the trees are leafless.

Some 500 species of plants and animals, including dozens of endangered species, depend on the aspen forest. It provides food for snowshoe hares, mice, and voles.

When snow falls, deer and elk nibble on aspen leaves, twigs, and bark. Grouse and quail dine on the winter buds. Black bears depend on aspen buds and foliage for food each spring. As young saplings stretch toward the spring sun, beavers cut them down for building their lodges. Mountain bluebirds, warbling vireos, and flycatchers nest in aspens, while birds of prey perch on snags of damaged trees waiting to catch their next meal.

ANIMAL LIFE

As with plant life, the varieties of animals in a region differ greatly with the land. The plains were once home to vast herds of large grazing beasts, such as deer, bison, and pronghorn. Today, black-tailed prairie dogs, swift foxes, and both greater and lesser prairie chickens inhabit the remaining grasslands. Burrowing owls nest in abandoned prairie dog holes. Grasslands also support mice, voles, and shrews, which, in turn, become prey for foxes, coyotes, and gray wolves.

Mountain regions have black bears. Agile otters, martens, weasels, and mink slip through streams and forests with ease. Badgers, the largest members of the weasel family, feed on pocket gophers, rats, and mice. The state's rivers and streams are home to cutthroat trout and a variety of suckers and chubs. The fish and their eggs provide food for dozens of species that come to the rivers to drink and feed. Beavers have made a strong comeback since fur trapping declined, and beaver families industriously gnaw down trees to build their lodges.

Black-tailed prairie dogs are among the many animals living in Colorado's grasslands.

COLORADO'S ENDANGERED SPECIES

Colorado has many animal and plant species that are in danger of becoming extinct. These species struggle to survive because they have been hunted, trapped for fur, or poisoned, or they have lost habitats. Animal species affected only in Colorado include seven species of frogs and toads, 19 species of birds, 23 species of fish, 13 mammals, 10 reptiles, and 2 mollusks.

Some species—whooping cranes, gray wolves, black-footed ferrets, and razorback suckers—are federally endangered species. They are in danger of extinction throughout the United States, not just in Colorado. Birds of prey such as bald eagles, American peregrine falcons, lesser prairie chickens, and burrowing owls have made progress toward recovery in Colorado. Some state endangered species have interesting names such as boreal toads, plains sharp-tailed grouse, and northern redbelly dace.

Mountain goats, deer, elk, moose, and bighorn sheep feed in mountain meadows and on scraggly tufts of grass on cliffs. These large plant eaters become food for large meat eaters: bears, wolves, and mountain lions.

In the cliffs and canyons, sharp-eyed ferruginous hawks and peregrine falcons wait for prey to appear on the scene. The hawks prefer rabbits, hares, prairie dogs, and ground squirrels for dinner. Swift, powerful flyers, falcons snatch other birds in mid-flight. Hunting at dawn or dusk, falcons hope for swallows, swifts, and rock wrens on their menus.

ENVIRONMENTAL ISSUES

Taking care of the environment is a major political and economic issue in Colorado. Keeping wilderness areas wild, controlling urban sprawl, and ensuring fresh, clean lakes and rivers are important.

In 2003, the U.S. government stopped protecting more than 600,000 acres (242,811 ha) of Colorado wilderness, putting its flora, fauna, and ancient artwork in danger of being damaged by development. Private and public government programs have preserved the James Peak Wilderness, Canyons of the Ancients National Monument, and the Spanish Peaks Wilderness. But in 2007, untouched places such as Vermillion Basin, Grape Creek, and Bull Gulch were still at risk.

Lack of rain results in drought, an extended period of dryness. Drought leaves prairie and forest lands dry and vulnerable to wildfire. Animals and plants suffer from the lack of water. The solution

Gray wolf

is smart water planning, such as investing in universal water **conservation**, a plan that affects all people in the state, not just those in dry areas. But controlling the water system and making it more efficient is expensive.

Coloradans and their government are concerned about pollution in the air and water. The state looks to limit and reduce pollution where it starts. For example, greenhouses in the state produce seedlings, flowers, and vegetable starter sets. Greenhouses also create a fair amount of pollution through the use of fertilizers and **pesticides**, which enter the soil when the plants are watered. Colorado's nurseries limit their use of these potentially harmful substances to reduce pollution outside the greenhouses.

Coloradans take pride in the natural variety of their state. Many are actively involved in conservation efforts to ensure the survival of Colorado's magnificent mountains, lakes, and forests. From the sweeping plains of the east to the sage-strewn desert in the west, Colorado is a picture postcard come to life.

WORDS TO KNOW

conservation *the act of saving or preserving something, such as a natural resource, plant, or animal species*

pesticides *any chemicals or biological agents used to kill plant or animal pests*

Water is scarce in some areas of Colorado. It is important to keep sources of water clean for humans and wildlife.

READ ABOUT

Bison were an important source of food for people of Colorado for thousands of years.

10,000 BCE
Humans arrive in Colorado

3000–500 BCE ▲
Village and farming culture develops in some areas of the Southwest

100 BCE
Ancient Puebloan culture emerges in Colorado

CHAPTER TWO

FIRST PEOPLE

★

WHEN HUMANS FIRST ARRIVED IN COLORADO 12,000 YEARS AGO, THE LAND TEEMED WITH HUGE ANIMALS. Bison roamed in herds on the grassy plains, along with elk, deer, antelope, and a relative of the modern-day horse. People hunted megafauna for meat and gathered what roots, berries, and nuts they could find to eat in their hunting area.

▲600–1300 CE
Ancient Puebloans occupied Mesa Verde

1300▲
Ancient Puebloan culture disappears

1300–1500
Jicarilla Apaches move into Colorado

Corn was a critical crop for early Coloradans.

EARLY PEOPLES

Eventually, the large animals decreased in numbers and died out. This may have been because of climate changes, overhunting, or both. Whatever the reason, hunter-gatherers had to make important changes. About 4,000 years ago, some people in the Southwest began planting crops—corn, beans, and squash—and forming villages. They used sharpened stones for spearheads or knives, wooden tools as shovels for digging roots, and rounded stones to grind corn or seeds into meal.

Hurling a spear with a thrower, called an atlatl, added enough speed and force to bring down deer, mountain sheep, or antelope. Although these early people were highly successful, they, too, disappeared.

Native American Peoples

(Before European Contact)

This map shows the general area of Native American peoples before European settlers arrived.

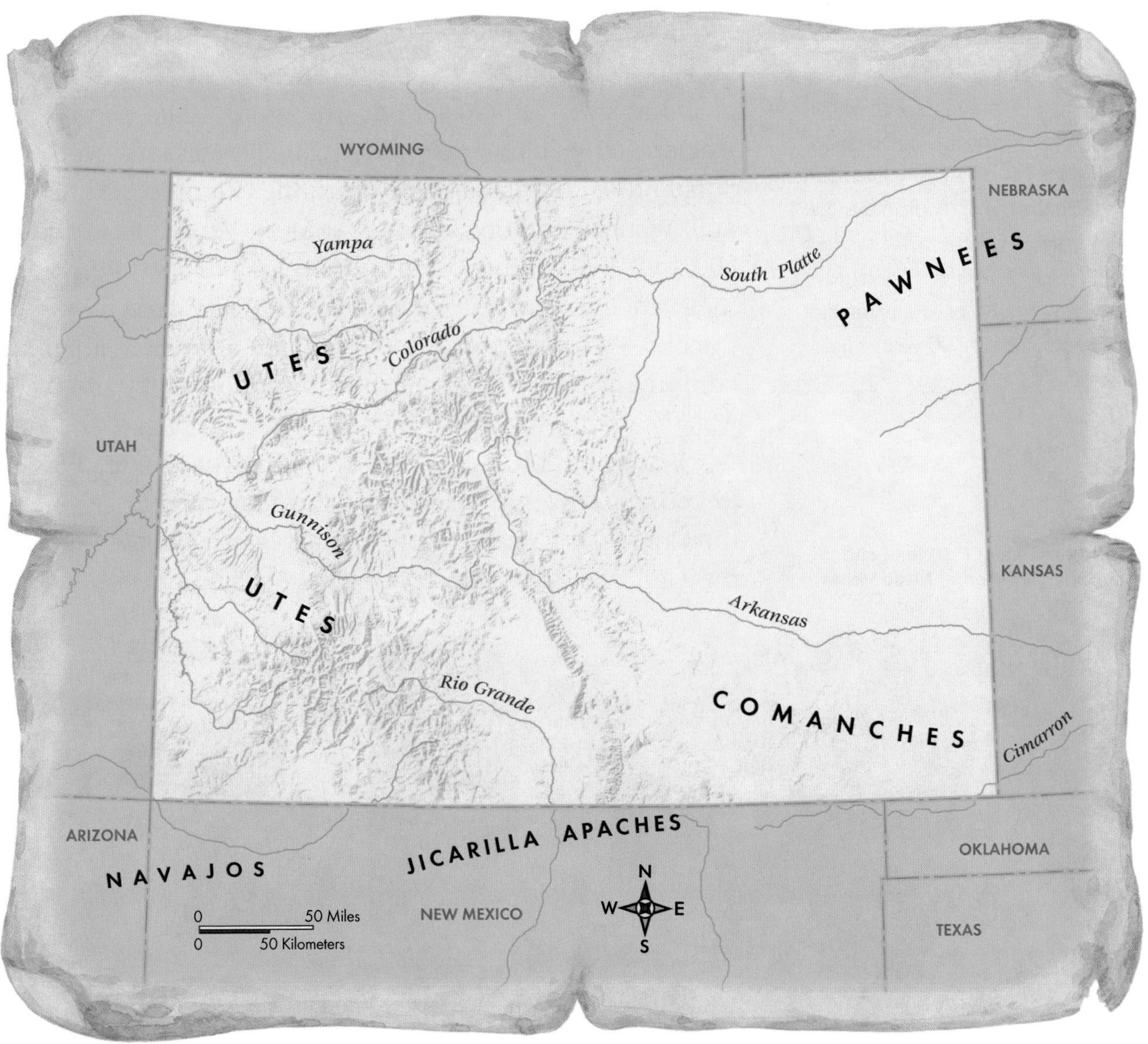

SEE IT HERE!

CROW CANYON

From June through September, Crow Canyon offers a hands-on, working tour of an Ancient Puebloan archaeological site. Participants get a real taste of what it is like to clear a site, preserve artifacts, and learn about the history of a nation that disappeared about 700 years ago.

THE ANCIENT PUEBLOANS

A different group of Native people had emerged in the southwestern United States by around 100 BCE. They also farmed corn, beans, and squash, but added tamed turkeys to their diet. They gathered fruit, nuts, and roots, and hunted and fished. They wove sturdy baskets for collecting and storing food, and made pottery of many sizes to hold liquids and grains. The people, Ancient Puebloans (formerly called Anasazi), were outstanding architects. One stunning example of their architectural abilities is found at Mesa Verde. Between 600 and 1300 CE, they built more than 4,000 structures there, including an elaborate four-story city carved into the cliffs, without power tools or large animals to haul equipment. They believed the sun brought life, and it was the center of their religion.

Between 1200 and 1300 CE, something happened that forced the Ancient Puebloans to abandon their cities on the Colorado Plateau. Many archaeologists believe that they left the area because of drought or famine.

Ruins of the Ancient Puebloan cliff dwellings can be seen at Mesa Verde National Park.

UTES AND PAIUTES

At about the same time as the Ancient Puebloans, a group of native people called Utes also lived in Colorado. Originally, Utes were seven different forest-dwelling tribes that had lived throughout Colorado. But by this time, Utes lived mainly in the mountains and deserts of western Colorado. Those living in the mountains hunted and fished the plentiful game. They ate berries, fruits, and nuts that grew wild in the forests.

Ramadas provided very little protection from bad weather.

The desert dwellers hunted smaller game and tended to move more often to find new food sources. Some desert Ute families lived in huts, called wickiups, made from arched poles that they covered with bark, grass, or branches. Others lived in open-air shelters, called ramadas, made of upright poles covered with branches. Both wickiups and ramadas could be easily dismantled and reassembled for a quick move to another hunting site.

Utes believed they were closely related to the bear, an animal that is often featured in Ute legends. Ute shamans, or holy men, were believed to be very powerful.

Picture Yourself . . .

as a Paiute Buffalo Hunter

Autumn approaches. It is the time of the summer buffalo hunt. You will be included in the hunt for the first time, and as exciting as this is, you also realize that if the hunt fails, your people will go hungry this winter. As the hunters approach, the buffalo stampede. The thunder of hooves on the land vibrates through the air. The hunt is on. You have a job to do.

Each spring, Utes gathered for the annual Bear Dance, known as *Momaqui Mowat*. In the summer, Utes met for the Sun Dance, their most important social and religious ceremony.

Southern Paiutes were relatives of Utes. *Paiute* means "tree Ute" or "water Ute." The Paiute nation had two basic branches: Northern Paiutes lived in what are now California, Nevada, and Oregon; and Southern Paiutes lived in what are now Colorado, Arizona, and Utah. Both Southern Paiutes and Utes spoke similar languages. Southern Paiutes tended to be hunter-gatherers, living in temporary villages and following their prey. They also settled along rivers long enough to plant, raise, and harvest crops. Typical Paiute crops included corn, squash, melons, gourds, and sunflowers. It was among Southern Paiutes that the Ghost Dance, a religious movement, became popular in the late 1800s. It represented the hope of the people to return to their past, a time when they lived without white people taking their land and killing the buffalo.

JICARILLA APACHES

On the high plains to the east, Jicarilla Apaches and Arapahos lived along Colorado's main rivers. Jicarilla Apaches migrated from Canada between 1300 and 1500 CE. They settled along the Arkansas River, in the southern Colorado mountains, and in upper New Mexico. Like other Native American groups, Jicarilla Apaches hunted and fished, gathered fruits, nuts, and roots, and changed camps with the seasons. They were such skilled basket weavers that Spanish explorers called them Jicarillas, which means "little baskets."

Apaches believed in one main Creator, called Ussen, and in several lesser gods. Some of these lesser gods, called *ga'ns*, are protective spirits. The Apache religion has a creation story that includes a flood. The religion also has four sacred colors: black, blue, yellow, and white. These colors guided Apaches as they prayed to the Creator. During creation, the Creator used his sweat to make other gods, the heavens, Earth, plants, and animals.

Bison were a primary resource for Jicarilla Apaches. The bison provided meat, and its skin was used to make coverings for tepees. **Sinew** was used for sewing as well as in hunting bows; bones became tools for pounding or grinding grains into flour.

When the Spanish first explored Colorado, they encountered Native American villagers who were healthy, productive, and proud. The Spanish, with their metal armor, horses, and weapons, were at first a source of great interest to Colorado's Native people. They could not have anticipated that the Spanish were only the first in what became an endless flow of foreigners into their homelands.

Jicarilla Apaches were known for their expert basket weaving.

WORD TO KNOW

sinew *an inflexible cord or band of connective tissue that joins muscle to bone*

READ ABOUT

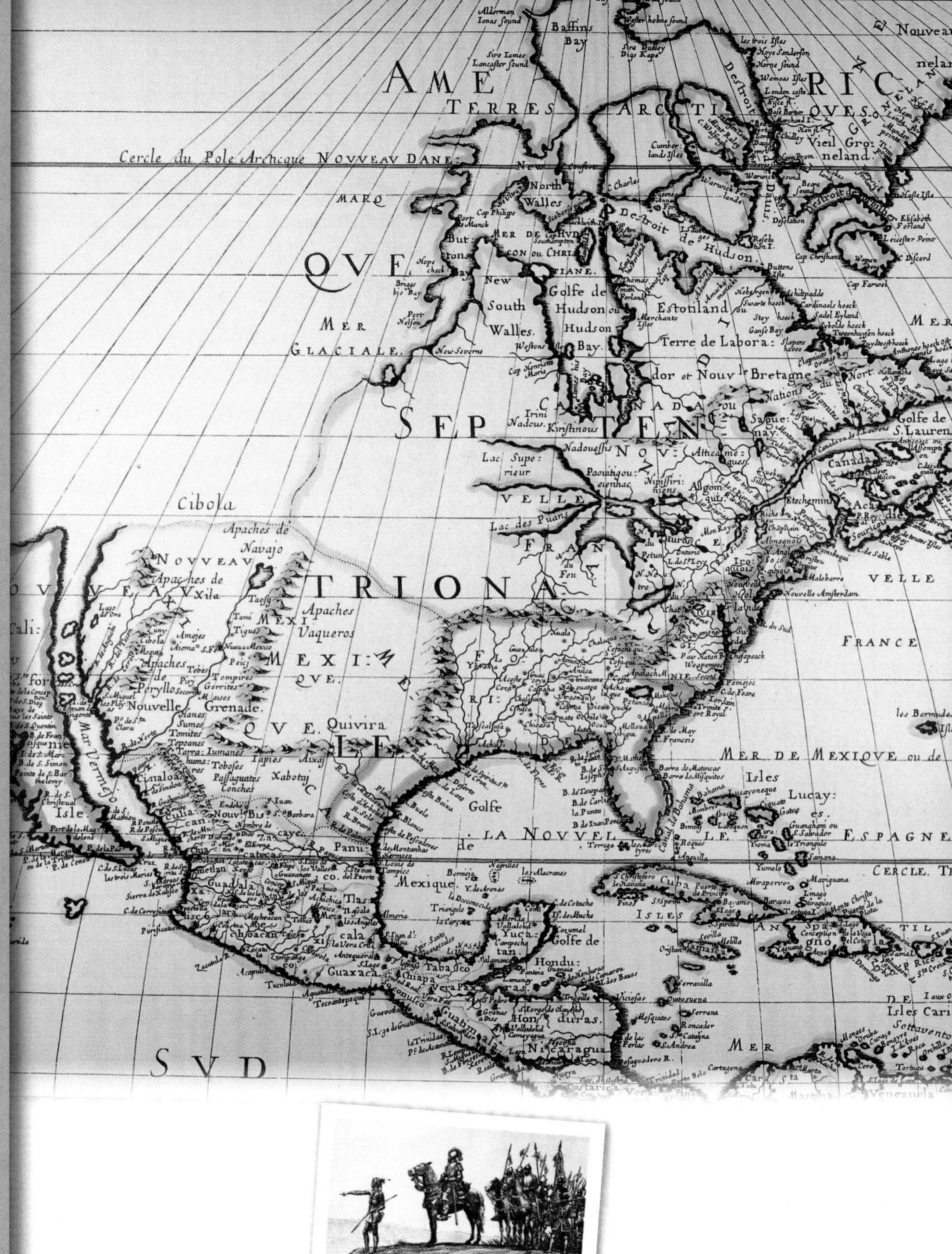

This map from 1650 includes the general location where Cíbola was believed to be located.

1539
Estevanico opens the American Southwest to foreign exploration

1540–1543
Coronado leads an expedition through the Southwest

1720
Pedro de Villasur investigates French dealings in Colorado

EXPLORATION AND SETTLEMENT

★

IN 1539, A NORTH AFRICAN NAMED ESTEVANICO SERVED AS A SCOUT FOR AN EXPEDITION LED BY MARCOS DE NIZA, AN ITALIAN PRIEST, WHO WAS SEARCHING FOR RICHES IN THE LEGENDARY SEVEN CITIES OF CÍBOLA. As he pushed into uncharted territories for Europeans, Estevanico established friendly relations with Native Americans. His daring adventures opened the Southwest to foreign exploration.

1776
Domínguez and Vélez de Escalante seek a route to California

1806 ▸
Zebulon Pike leads a U.S. military expedition into eastern Colorado

1833
Mexican settlers receive land grants in Colorado

CONQUISTADORS ARRIVE

Following in Estevanico's footsteps, in 1540 Spanish **conquistador** Francisco Vásquez de Coronado led an expedition into the Southwest. Coronado's force included Europeans and enslaved Africans, some of whom escaped to join Native villagers in New Mexico, Arizona, and Colorado. Coronado, too, was searching for the Seven Cities of Cíbola, rumored to be filled with gold and silver. His expedition did not find gold, silver, or gems, but they did meet Native American peoples, including Utes and Comanches.

A Spanish army, wearing armor, riding on horses, and carrying unfamiliar weapons, confronted Native villagers. The Spanish must have frightened local tribes, and the tribes reacted by trying to protect their land the best way they knew. They faced the Spanish with spears and bows and arrows.

WORD TO KNOW

conquistador *one who conquers; specifically a leader in the Spanish conquest of the Americas*

MINI-BIO

FRANCISCO VÁSQUEZ DE CORONADO: CONQUISTADOR

Born in Salamanca, Spain, Francisco Vásquez de Coronado (1510–1554) was a Spanish conquistador who arrived in Mexico in 1535. From 1538 to 1544, he served as governor of Nueva Galicia, a Spanish colony in Mexico. From 1540 to 1542, he explored the Southwest. First he headed north from Nueva Galicia into what is now Arizona, and then he headed east, over the Rockies, and into Apache land on the Great Plains. During that time, he led an unsuccessful expedition in search of gold and silver. Coronado's search ended at a Wichita Native American village somewhere in today's Kansas. Discouraged, he returned to Nueva Galicia, where Native Americans rebelled against harsh Spanish rule. Coronado lost his position as governor and retired to live in Mexico City.

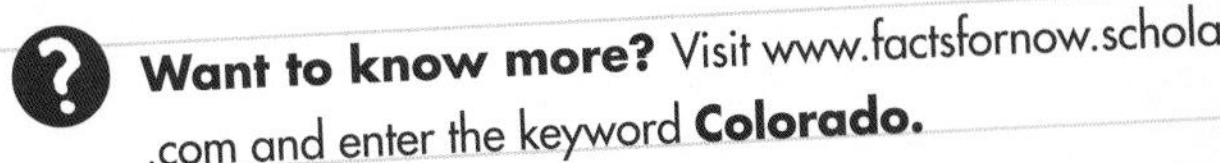

Want to know more? Visit www.factsfornow.scholastic.com and enter the keyword **Colorado.**

Members of Coronado's expedition

Exploration of Colorado

The colored arrows on this map show the routes taken by explorers between 1598 and 1844.

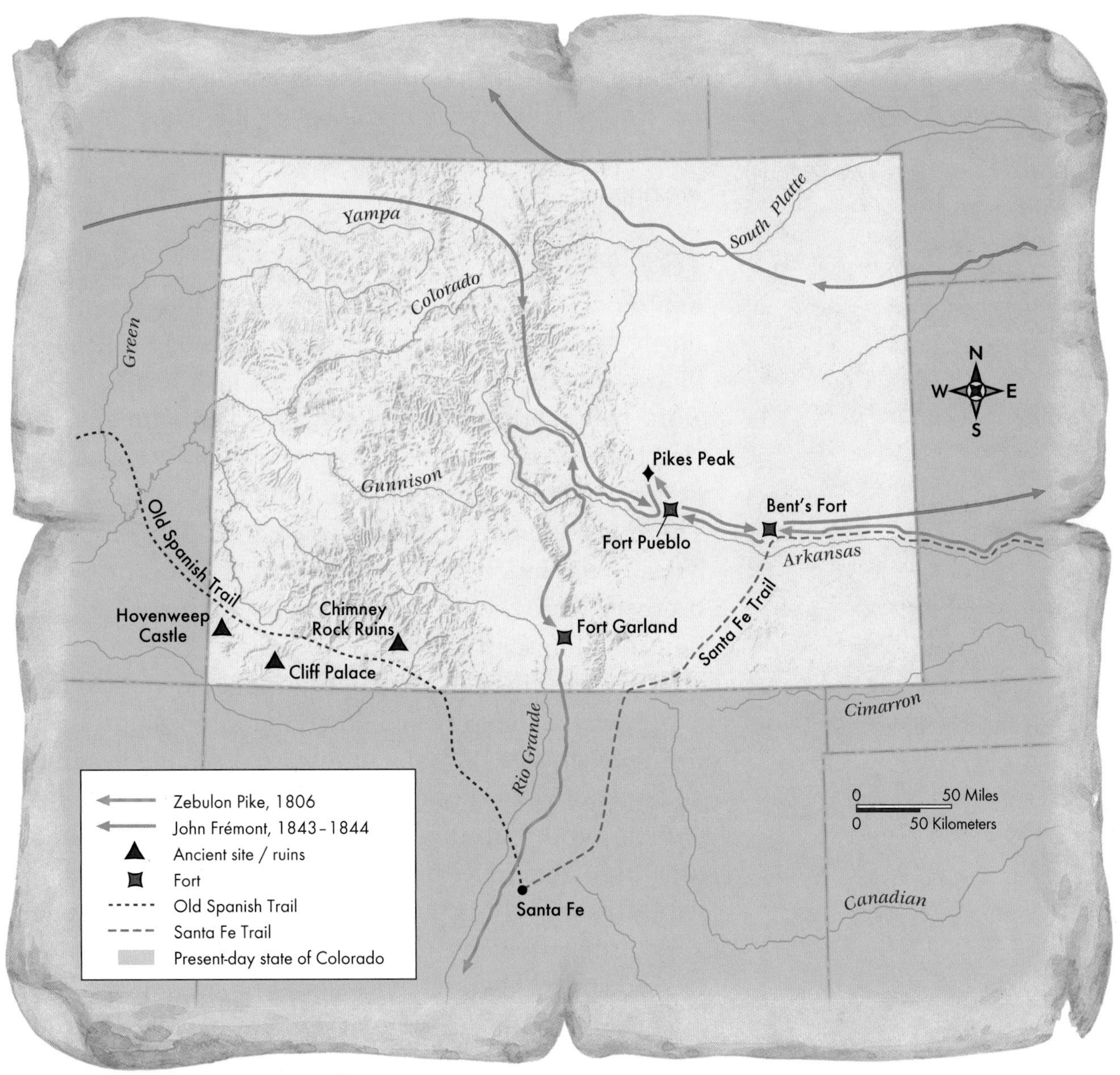

WHAT WERE THE SPANISH IN SEARCH OF?

Cities of gold, known as the Seven Cities of Cíbola. According to legend, seven Catholic bishops fled Portugal in 714 CE with a group of followers to escape invading Muslims. They headed across the Atlantic Ocean, supposedly to the land of Antilia and luxurious cities with great riches. Spanish conquistadors in the 1500s thought that islands in the Caribbean were the legendary Antilia, but that was not true. After many expeditions throughout southwestern North America—including Colorado and parts of Mexico—the Spanish finally gave up their hopes. There were no cities of gold or buildings of silver, only villages with crops of golden squash and dwellings of adobe.

THE SPANISH DEPART

The Spanish decided that settling in Colorado was too dangerous for too little reward. Colorado had challenging mountains and bitter winter weather. Native people were hostile toward them.

Although the land was scenic, the Spanish did not find what they wanted most—gold. They built no settlements or missions, as they did in Texas and New Mexico.

THE FRENCH

Explorers from France entered Colorado from the north, and they were in search of riches of a different kind—beavers. In Europe, the most fashionable men wore hats made from beaver pelts. The women carried beaver muffs (tubes of fur that kept their hands warm), and they had beaver collars on their coats. These fashion demands proved so great that Europe's beaver population had become extinct, and European trappers were well on their way to eliminating millions of American beavers.

In 1682, French explorer René-Robert Cavelier, Sieur de La Salle, traveled down the Mississippi River from present-day Illinois southward. La Salle declared all land between the Rocky and the Allegheny mountains to be the property of France. Named Louisiana for King Louis XIV, this vast territory included about two-fifths of what is now Colorado. But this claim had very little effect on Colorado; most Native peoples never even knew the land was in French hands.

In 1706, Juan de Uribarri led an expedition into southwest Colorado and claimed it for Spain. That area became a part of Spain's New Mexico territory, under the rule of the Spanish governor in Santa Fe.

René-Robert Cavelier, Sieur de La Salle, claiming the Louisiana Territory for France in 1682

Spain became concerned that French fur traders were trespassing on Spanish soil. The Spanish did not want the French to become rich trapping beavers and other furs on Spanish claims. In 1720, Pedro de Villasur headed north into Colorado to find out about rumored French settlements and trading posts. He met a band of Pawnees. Villasur, 34 of his soldiers, and 11 of his scouts were killed.

A thousand miles (1,600 km) to the east, the French and Indian War (1754–1763) took place—which, despite the distance, affected Colorado. The war pitted the French and several allied Native

Native Americans traded animal furs and other goods with European settlers.

American nations against the British. Eastern North America had been settled by both the French and the British for more than 100 years when the war began. The two countries were fighting over the Ohio Valley. British citizens wanted to move into the Ohio Valley to farm the rich soil of that region, but the French laid claim to the area. The French believed that British settlers threatened the riches gained from trapping furs in the valley. When the British won the war, France ceded its Great Plains lands east of the Mississippi to Great Britain, and some of its western lands to Spain. Eastern Colorado became Spanish again.

Once again, Spanish treasure seekers headed into Colorado. Juan Maria de Rivera led a group into the Sangre de Cristo and the San Juan mountains, looking for silver and gold. Their mining successes were minimal, but Rivera did become the first European to explore the region along the Gunnison River.

Farther west, the Spanish had established a thriving colony in California. But transportation between colonies was difficult. Because the Colorado River cut very deep canyons across the Southwest, the Spanish looked for an easier route from Santa Fe to California. Francisco Domínguez and Silvestre Vélez de Escalante headed northward to find such a route in 1776. The explorers became lost and would have died of thirst if a Ute man hadn't found them and led them to water. Domínguez and Escalante never were able to cross the land's deep canyons.

Louisiana Purchase

This map shows the area (in yellow) that made up the Louisiana Purchase and the present-day state of Colorado (in orange).

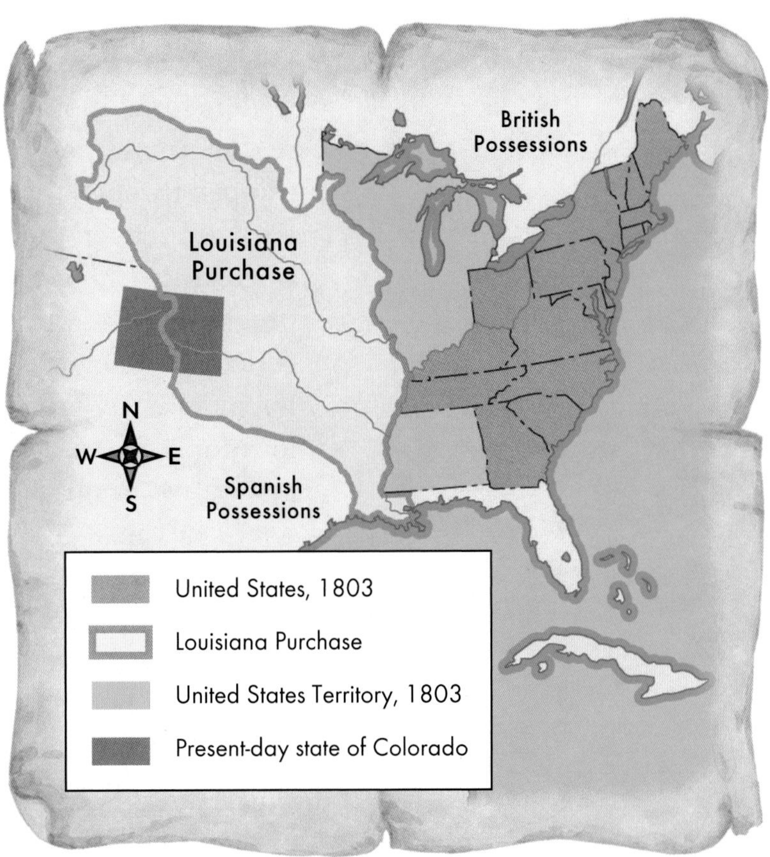

In 1800, France regained control of the Louisiana Territory, only to turn around and sell it to the United States in 1803. In 1806, the U.S. government sent Lieutenant Zebulon Pike to explore what it had bought in eastern Colorado. On this journey, he mapped what would be known as Pikes Peak, which became a destination for settlers moving west and is today the most-climbed mountain in Colorado.

TRADERS AND TRAPPERS

The early 1800s brought many more traders and trappers to the Colorado Rockies. Traders brought blankets, weapons, or liquor to exchange with Native Americans for furs. The demand for fur was so great that European traders hired mountain men to trap for them as well.

Mountain men were rugged, solitary people. They trapped throughout the winter, often spending months away from even the smallest trading post. In Colorado, Auguste P. Chouteau organized a large-scale trapping program. His trappers met yearly to swap tall tales, collect supplies for the next year, and trade their furs for money. Colorado trappers usually met at a central location that could handle a large number of campers, Native Americans, and traders, such as Bear Creek near Denver.

In 1829, Missouri brothers William and Charles Bent guided a wagon train along the Santa Fe Trail, and the idea for a new business was born. The brothers established Bent's Fort in 1833 near the Arkansas River. It was a rectangular adobe building with a blacksmith shop, general store, and an icehouse. Soon, trading posts sprang up along well-traveled routes, usually near rivers. These posts doubled as forts, offering goods for trade in peaceful times and protection against attacks in violent ones.

Although trapping and trading brought many whites to Colorado, few mountain men were interested in developing permanent settlements. The first white settlers came in 1851, when José Jacques brought his family and five others from Mexico to the San Luis Valley to live. They established ranches, where they raised cattle and farmed crops to feed their livestock and themselves.

A Mexican American family poses for a photograph beside their adobe home on a ranch in Costilla County in the late 1800s.

These six Mexican families had received a land grant in 1833, but they did not establish a settlement at that time. Then war broke out between Mexico and the United States in 1846. When the war ended two years later, the families moved onto the land they were originally granted, and the new settlement, near Conejos, became the first permanent white settlement in Colorado.

READ ABOUT

This engraving shows Cherry Creek as it appeared in 1860, after gold was discovered in the area.

1858 ▲
Gold is discovered in Colorado

1861–1865
Civil War affects the new Colorado territory

1867
Treaty of Medicine Lodge is signed

CHAPTER FOUR

GROWTH AND CHANGE

★

GOLD—AT LAST! In 1858, William Russell discovered gold on Cherry Creek. When word of gold spread, miners swarmed into Denver and the surrounding mountains. Named for the governor of Kansas Territory, Denver then was a crude settlement of wooden buildings, tents, muddy streets, and general stores.

1870
Railroad line opens to Denver

1876 ►
Colorado gains statehood

1893
Colorado grants women the right to vote

MINI-BIO

JAMES BECKWOURTH: MOUNTAIN MAN

James Beckwourth (1798–1866) began life enslaved in Virginia but was raised in St. Louis, Missouri. He watched others heading west and dreamed of adventure. In 1823, he became involved in fur trading in the Rocky Mountains. Later he served as a guide, trapper, trader, army scout, and hunter. He discovered a pass through the Sierra Nevada, which was later named after him. The pass made traveling to California's Sacramento Valley easier during the California gold rush. Beckwourth settled in Denver late in life. His autobiography, *Life and Adventures of James P. Beckwourth*, describes the life of the frontiersmen known as mountain men.

Want to know more? Visit www.factsfornow.scholastic.com and enter the keyword **Colorado.**

BUILDING TOWNS

In 1859, John Gregory found gold near Central City, and 40,000 prospectors rushed to Colorado. Many painted signs on the sides of their wagons reading "Pike's Peak or Bust!" Those prospectors had no idea that Pikes Peak was not gold country.

Mining towns sprang up at every convenient location. New Colorado towns included Central City, Breckenridge, and Telluride. The towns were ungoverned, rugged, and filthy. Miners filed claims on pieces of land that they would mine. A claim was supposed to show legal ownership of the land. Miners lived near their claims because leaving the claim could mean losing it. Miners' courts sprang up to work out differences between miners over claim rights, partnership problems, and other legal disagreements.

Because miners were busy panning or digging for gold, they needed services such as laundries, bathhouses, restaurants, boardinghouses, blacksmiths, and general stores. The area had few women, but those who went to Colorado provided some of these services, as well as housekeeping, and they were paid in gold dust. One of these women, Ellen E. Hunt, set up a small dairy and bakery: "I sell the milk at 10¢ per quart

WOW

Prospectors sometimes used gold dust instead of coins. A pinch of dust between the thumb and forefinger was equal to 25¢.

A view of Breckenridge's main street in the 1880s

and make $2.75 a day. My butter brought $1.00 per lb. and balls of smearcase [cottage cheese] 40¢ per doz. . . Weary days of labor and pain. Have made 175 loaves of bread and 450 pies. Taken all the care of the children and done all the housework but the washing." Women such as Hunt worked hard for their money, but many earned more than the miners who bought their goods. Some became fairly wealthy.

While merchants made high profits, miners did not fare so well. Many ran out of money and struggled to return home. In an article entitled "Pike's Peak Gold Mines," one author described the failed miners: "During the past ten days we have met thousands of the deluded and suffering gold-seekers retracing their steps to the quiet farms of the West. Many of them were in a starving condition, barefooted, ragged, and penniless; and it has caused much delay in the progress of the expedition, and materially diminished our supply of provisions to feed these hungry, home-bound strollers."

Q8 HOW DID MINERS SEPARATE GOLD FROM ROCK?

A8 There were two ways of getting gold out of rock. Panning for gold in a moving stream or river was called placer mining. The gold dust was heavier than most rock, and swishing river gravel around in water separated the gold from the waste. Digging underground looking for a vein of gold in rock was called lode mining, which involved elaborate tunnels and heavy equipment. The first required patience and a large pan and was often practiced by individuals; the second required a pick and shovel and a strong back and was often organized by mining companies with many laborers.

GROWING COLORADO

Gold mining towns developed into cities, and soon settlers spread out onto the plains and the western slopes. Because of the increase in population, the U.S. Congress made Colorado a territory in 1861. A territory was an area that belonged to the United States but had not yet met the requirements for becoming a state. Territories applied for statehood, which had to be approved by the U.S. Congress; then the president could declare it a state.

As Denver grew, clashes between Native Americans and white settlers increased. By this time, additional Native groups had also arrived in the state, among them Arapahos, Cheyennes, and Kiowas who had been hunting and living in the eastern part of the state. Whites took Native land, abused Native Americans' rights, and killed buffalo, an animal essential to their way of life. Cattle ranchers claimed large areas for cattle grazing.

A man pans for gold in Clear Creek County

Native Americans did not believe in the idea of owning land. They found the settlers' customs strange. Why fence in land that belongs to everyone? They resented being pushed around, and they fought back.

THE CIVIL WAR

Colorado had been a territory for only a few weeks when the American Civil War (1861–1865) broke out between the antislavery North and the pro-slavery South. In addition to people who had permanently settled in Colorado, the territory's residents included both Northerners and Southerners. Some returned to their home states to sign up for the Union (Northern) or Confederate (Southern) armies. Those who remained in Colorado fought on the Union side of the war.

In Colorado, officially a Union territory, the territorial governor organized regiments that headed into New Mexico and Kansas. They fought in the battles of Apache Canyon, Pigeon's Ranch, and Peralta. When the Union finally won the war in 1865, Colorado soldiers returned to seek jobs in ranching, mining, and industry. Many newly freed slaves headed west, looking for new lives and new opportunities. Some found jobs as cowboys, farmers, and shopkeepers.

SEE IT HERE!

RIDE 'EM, COWBOY!

The first rodeo was held on July 4, 1869, in Deer Trail on the eastern plains. Today, Denver hosts one of the world's largest annual rodeos, the National Western Stock Show. Rodeos give cowboys and cowgirls a chance to show their skills roping calves, riding horses, and taming bucking broncos. The stock show's mission is to preserve the western lifestyle and draw attention to the cattle industry in Colorado. Even children get in on the act. Five- to seven-year-olds weighing less than 55 pounds (25 kilograms) can ride a sheep out of a chute and into the arena in the Mutton Bustin' event. Don't worry, the kids wear helmets and padding, and the sheep are well protected by their heavy wool coats.

THE SAND CREEK MASSACRE

By the 1860s, Denver's citizens were determined to force Native American nations off their Colorado lands. Governor William Gilpin and *Rocky Mountain News* editor William Byers began a campaign to arouse anger and hatred toward Native Americans, regardless of whether they were peaceful or not.

Cheyenne chief Black Kettle, in an attempt to keep peace, agreed that his people would camp with

A painting of the Sand Creek Massacre in 1864

Arapahos under Chief Left Hand at Sand Creek, north of the Arkansas River in eastern Colorado. Black Kettle was given an American flag, a white flag, and a pledge that waving these flags showed peaceful intentions and would keep the camp safe.

Colonel John M. Chivington, a military leader and Protestant minister, argued against a treaty with Cheyennes and advocated killing them. He organized his cavalry and other volunteers, and at dawn on November 29, 1864, they attacked Sand Creek. Black Kettle waved his flags, but his plea for peace was ignored. The troops massacred around 170 Indian women, children, and elderly. Cheyenne and Arapaho men fought back, allowing nearly 500 to escape, including Black Kettle. The Sand Creek Massacre was one of the most shameful acts against Native Americans in the history of the United States. Eventually, the U.S. Congress investigated and publicly criticized Chivington. Though he was never formally charged with a crime, he was forced to resign.

With the signing of the 1867 Treaty of Medicine Lodge, the Cheyenne and Arapaho were forced to give up their Colorado lands and move to a **reservation** in Oklahoma. That same year, Denver was made the capital of the territory.

MINI-BIO

CHRISTOPHER "KIT" CARSON: WILD WEST LEGEND

Christopher "Kit" Carson (1809–1868) had several careers: mountain man, fur trapper, and guide. Born in Kentucky and raised in Missouri, Carson left home at age 16 to see the West. For 15 years, he roamed the Rocky Mountains trapping animals. He guided John C. Frémont, an explorer and champion of the expansion of the United States from coast to coast, through the Rockies to California in 1842. As a member of the army, Kit Carson led U.S. troops against the Navajos, destroying their crops, orchards, and livestock. He retired from military life in 1867 and died a year later.

Want to know more? Visit www.factsfornow.scholastic.com and enter the keyword **Colorado.**

BUFFALO SOLDIERS

African American soldiers of the 9th and 10th cavalry regiments were among the U.S. troops sent to Colorado to keep the peace between settlers and Indian nations. Famed frontiersman Kit Carson served as a scout for the 9th Cavalry when they were stationed at Fort Garland in Colorado.

These troops were nicknamed Buffalo Soldiers by Cheyenne warriors, in part, out of respect for their fierce fighting ability. They made up 20 percent of the entire U.S. Cavalry in the West and earned 18 Congressional Medals of Honor for their heroism.

For black soldiers, though, fighting Native Americans could often be a wrenching experience. They wanted to help their country, but many blacks were of mixed Indian and African ancestry. They had to carry out orders by government officials and their

WORD TO KNOW

reservation *land set aside for a group to live on, usually Native Americans*

white officers to keep Native Americans on reservations. And they were part of a U.S. military effort that allowed whites to seize Indian lands.

ROAD TO STATEHOOD

Technological advances slowly made their way to Colorado from the East. The transcontinental **telegraph** system was completed by 1861, and the first telegraph arrived in Julesburg, Colorado, that same year. By 1875, most of the state was connected by wire. That year, silver was found in Leadville, and a new prospecting "rush" was on. Three years later, telephones came to Denver, although it would be years before anyone in Denver could call New York or Boston.

WORD TO KNOW

telegraph *a means of communication through which messages were sent along wires using a code of long and short (dashes and dots) pulses*

The first schoolhouse in Colorado was built in Boulder in 1860.

White settlers controlled the eastern section of Colorado, and Utes controlled the west. In 1879, a U.S. Indian agent, Nathan Meeker, and his party were slain by Utes. During this time, Utes had a dynamic, intelligent leader in Chief Ouray. Ouray recognized that U.S. power could overcome his people, and he arranged a peace treaty. Utes agreed to move to reservations in Utah and southwestern Colorado. The land they left was quickly occupied by white farmers and cattle ranchers.

Ranchers, miners, and merchants, including immigrants who had come to Colorado seeking work, helped build Colorado. John Henderson had started the first Colorado cattle ranch in 1859, the year of the Colorado gold rush. John Wesley Iliff, the "cattle king of the Plains," became Colorado's first cattle baron with a herd of 50,000 head. The Transcontinental Railroad, which joined the eastern and western parts of the United States, was completed in 1869. Built in large part by immigrants, including many Chinese and Irish laborers, the Transcontinental Railroad included a feeder line to Denver within a year. This made the area more accessible to people from across the country. As the population grew, Coloradans became anxious for statehood.

MINI-BIO

CHIEF OURAY: PEACEMAKER

Ute leader Chief Ouray (1833–1880) was born in New Mexico and spoke fluent Spanish. Both before being recognized as principal chief of the bands of Southern Utes in 1868 and after, he participated in discussions with the U.S. government about Ute lands. In 1868, Ouray and the Utes gave up their claims to central and far northwestern Colorado. Later they were forced out of most of the western part of the state. Today, some Utes remain on a small portion of their ancestral lands in southwestern Colorado, and others live in Utah.

Want to know more? Visit www.factsfornow.scholastic.com and enter the keyword **Colorado.**

ALL KINDS OF COWBOYS

Not all cowhands and cattle barons were white men. On the Colorado Plateau, Ann Bassett was a successful rancher who could ride and rope with the best cowboys. One-third of Colorado's cowboys were African American, Hispanic, or Native American. The word *buckaroo,* a term for cowboy, comes from the Spanish word *vaquero*.

Colorado traveled a bumpy road to becoming a state. In April 1859, white settlers attempted to make Colorado a sovereign, or self-governing, state. Although voters rejected this proposition, a temporary government was set up, and the area was called the Territory of Jefferson. Several times, the voters went to the polls to approve a constitution, and every time, the new version of the document was rejected.

Many people in the East did not want new states in the Wild West. The Pittsburgh *Commercial* reflected these opinions: "There is something repulsive that a few handfuls of rough miners and reckless bullwhackers should have the same voice in the Senate as Pennsylvania, New York and Ohio."

In 1870, Colorado's population reached about 40,000. By 1875, the railroads had brought East Coast products to Colorado, and eastern opposition to western states had lessened. Colorado drew up another constitution, which passed 19,483 to 15,830 in 1876. A month later, President Ulysses S. Grant proclaimed Colorado a state. John Routt, a Republican, became the state's first governor.

When Colorado became a state, its constitution allowed men, both white and African American, to vote. However, neither women nor Native Americans could vote.

This didn't sit well with some women. Colorado had depended heavily on women to help tame the wilderness. Wives worked beside their husbands clearing farmland, raising cattle, and running businesses. In the late 1870s, Colorado's women received the right to vote in local school board elections. It took about another 15 years of hard work on the part of many organizers and leaders such as Ellis Meredith before

FAQ

Q: WHY IS COLORADO CALLED THE CENTENNIAL STATE?

A: Colorado became a state in 1876, when the United States was 100 years old. Centennial means 100 years, and the state's nickname honors that milestone in history.

Colorado: From Territory to Statehood

(1861–1876)

This map shows the original Colorado territory and the area (outlined in orange) that became the state of Colorado in 1876.

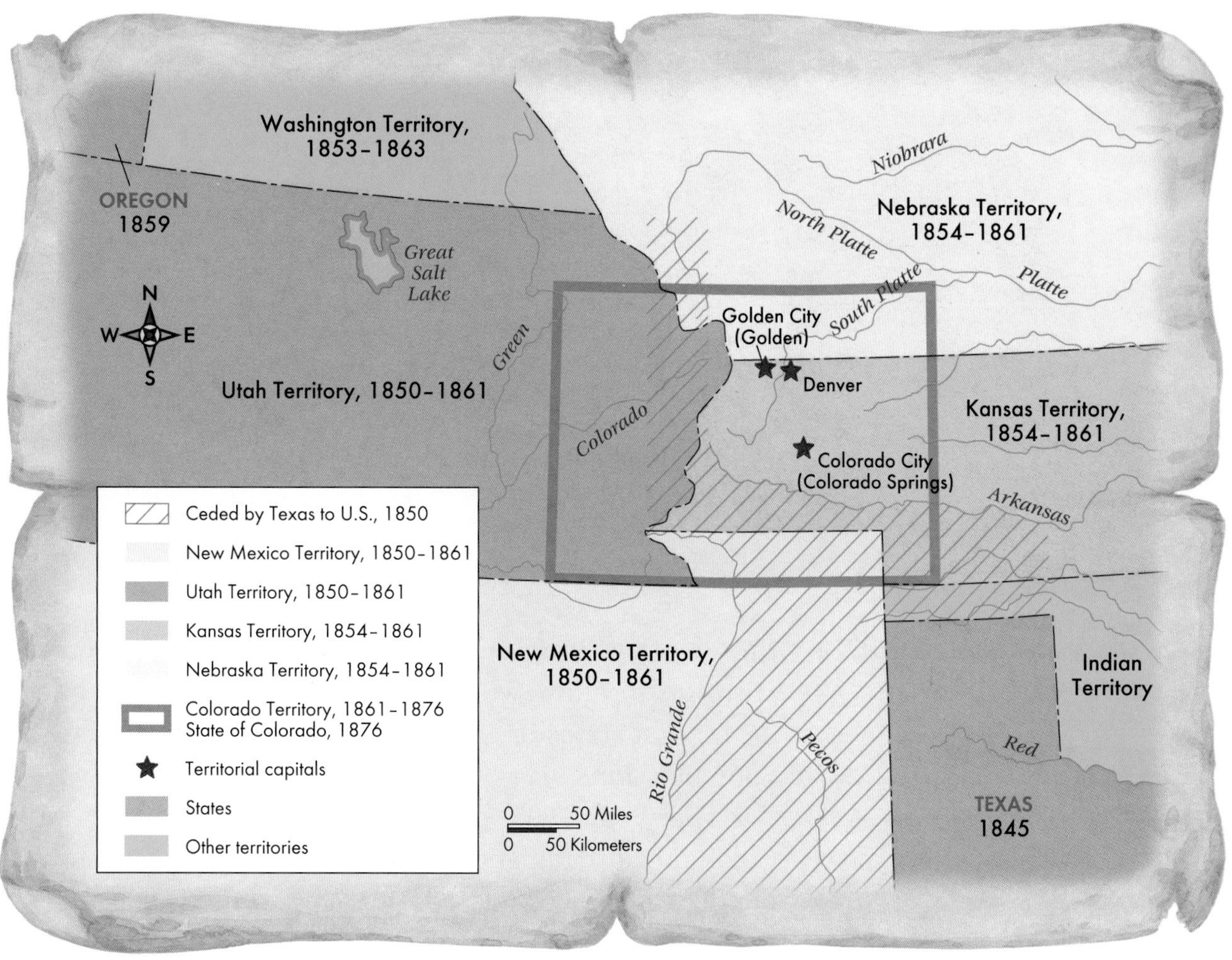

Men and women gather outside a Colorado polling place to vote in 1907.

WORDS TO KNOW

suffragists *people who worked to achieve voting and other civil rights for women*

depression *a long period during which productivity is low, many people are out of work, and the value of money is unstable*

the voters (all male) agreed to change the state constitution to allow women to vote. Colorado was one of the first states in which women could vote in statewide elections.

That year, 1893, proved to be a successful one for Colorado's **suffragists**, but not for its miners. Silver producing states like Colorado mined so much silver that the supply exceeded the demand leading to a decline in the price. As silver's value fell, many Colorado mines closed, and the state's economy went into a **depression**. In mining towns such as Leadville and Aspen, unemployment rose and businesses struggled. Some people left the state.

in Pioneer Colorado

What was it like to be a child in Colorado in pioneer days? See what a Cheyenne boy, a rancher's son, and a miner's daughter had to say:

Wikis, a Cheyenne boy, remembers what it was like living with his family in a camp. Growing up Cheyenne, Wikis had different responsibilities than a boy growing up in Denver.

We all played at living in camp. In these camps we did the things that older people do. A boy and girl pretended to be husband and wife, and lived in the lodge; the girl cooked and the boy went out hunting. Sometimes some of the boys pretended that they were buffalo, and showed themselves on the prairie a little way off, and other boys were hunters, and went out to chase the buffalo. We were too little to have horses, but the boys rode sticks, which they held between their legs, and lashed with their [riding whips] to make them go faster.

A. W. McHendrie was a child raised in a Colorado town. He tells about his school experience.

During the winter of 1887, school was held in a little one-story, one-room building, and one of the popular entertainments during that winter was a **spelling school** *which was always held on Friday night and which not only the school children, but the entire population in and around Springfield attended. They chose up sides, getting everybody into the game.*

Martha Todd talks about the life of young boys and girls.

Coal miners as a rule had big families. The family of five was a small family. But they went from there, but I wouldn't say how high they went. I don't really know. I've heard of families of 12 and 15 children. . . . There were no child labor laws in those days and young boys 11, 12, and 13 years old went into the mines. And the girls, just as soon as they were able to take care of a baby, were kept at home. They didn't get to go to school much.

As Coloradans were working to include women in the political process, the U.S. government made moves to exclude some immigrants from entering the country. The Chinese Exclusion Act of 1882 outlawed the immigration of Chinese laborers and denied citizenship to the Chinese already settled in the United States. Racial and immigration tensions would continue to affect the country and Colorado into the next century.

WORD TO KNOW

spelling school *similar to a spelling bee, with the added benefit of learning how to use new vocabulary*

READ ABOUT

Miners pose for a photograph at the head of a gold mine shaft in Cripple Creek around 1890.

1903
Colorado miners go on strike

▲**1917**
Colorado men join the fighting in World War I

1930s
State's national parks are improved by New Deal programs during the Great Depression

CHAPTER FIVE

MORE MODERN TIMES

★

AS COLORADO ENTERED THE 20TH CENTURY, GOLD CONTINUED TO DRIVE THE STATE'S ECONOMY. The Cripple Creek mining district, for example, produced about $20 million each year—about $480 million in 2006 money. But while mine owners got rich, mine workers did not. Few were happy about their jobs. In 1903, the Western Federation of Miners went on strike.

▲ **1942**
Internment camp for Japanese Americans opens in Colorado

1973
Denver schools are ordered to desegregate

1999
Shooting at Columbine High School occurs

Armed miners stand outside their tents in Trinidad in April 1914.

STRIKES IN THE NEWS

In 1913–1914, another Colorado mine strike made national news. More than 1,000 coal miners protested poor pay, long hours, and dangerous working conditions. On April 20, 1914, the National Guard opened fire on the miners' tents, torching some of them and destroying private property. A number of people died as a result, among them 11 children. This event was known as the Ludlow Massacre.

The U.S. Mint in Denver opened for business in 1906 and produced about 167 million gold and silver coins that year, totaling $27 million worth of money. Today, the mint produces more than 50 million coins daily.

The United States entered World War I (1914–1918) in 1917. As Colorado men volunteered to fight, farms and ranches increased wheat and cattle production for sale to the military. The war led to a new Colorado industry—mining molybdenum. This silvery-white metallic element, when combined with steel, makes a stronger metal that is more resistant to heat. It is used to make linings for rifle barrels and filaments for lightbulbs.

After the war, Coloradans faced high food and land prices. At the same time, people enjoyed higher wages and higher profits for agricultural products and manufactured goods. This period of **inflation** lasted for several years. Then, in October 1929, the New York Stock Exchange crashed, and many people around the world lost their jobs and their money.

The United States fell into the Great Depression. Businesses closed, leaving employees without work. They had no money to pay bills, so families lost their homes and farms. On the Great Plains, a drought added to the problem. Years of dry weather created a dust bowl out of land that normally produced corn, wheat, hay, and millet. Poverty and hunger became a way of life in the early 1930s.

President Franklin D. Roosevelt offered a relief program called the New Deal. The New Deal created agencies that put people to work. Works Progress Administration (WPA) projects were as small as town water fountains and as large as hospitals, bridges, or schoolhouses. The Civilian Conservation Corps (CCC) helped improve conditions at national parks, such as Mesa Verde National Park and Rocky Mountain National Park. CCC workers planted trees, cleared snow, and developed ways to limit **erosion**. Coloradans were working again.

WORLD WAR II

Although Colorado's economy improved, recovery was not complete until the United States entered World War II (1939–1945), after the Japanese attack on Pearl Harbor in 1941. The war changed Colorado. New military bases sprouted up throughout the state. Farms produced more agricultural products than ever before. While productivity and profitability increased, the state also saw a different type of federal facility—an internment camp for Japanese Americans.

WORDS TO KNOW

inflation *an increase in the supply of currency or credit relative to the amount of goods or services available, resulting in higher prices*

erosion *the gradual wearing away of rock or soil by physical breakdown, chemical solution, or water*

The first group of Japanese Americans arrive at the Granada train station on their way to the Amache internment camp in 1942.

Following the surprise Japanese attack, the U.S. government became fearful of the Japanese American population in California. Some government officials claimed that Japanese Americans posed a security threat, especially those living near the Pacific coast. These Americans were rounded up and forced to live in camps. An internment camp called Amache was opened in Granada, Colorado. It consisted of row upon row of low buildings in which families lived, often one family in only one or two rooms. Amache held more than 7,000 Japanese Americans.

Colorado governor Ralph Carr opposed this action. He believed that Japanese Americans should not be stripped of their rights, particularly those who were American citizens. However, the federal government did not agree, and the internment camp stayed full to capacity with Japanese Americans until the end of the war. It took the U.S. government more than 40 years to apologize. President Ronald Reagan signed the Civil Liberties Act of 1988, which paid $20,000 to each surviving internee.

The end of the war brought freedom to the Amache internees and the return of soldiers and sailors to Colorado. A postwar economic boom in the 1950s saw increases in jobs, military bases, and population numbers. The U.S. Air Force Academy was founded in Colorado Springs in 1954, adding a military academy to the state's many universities and colleges.

Following World War II, the United States entered a period called the Cold War. This was not a war of bombs and bullets, but of words and fear. The United States, Great Britain, France, and other nations allied against **Communist** nations. In Colorado, the U.S. Army built a special war room in a bunker 1,000 feet (305 m) under the Cheyenne Mountain, in Colorado Springs. This bunker housed the North American Aerospace Defense Command (NORAD), a center from which U.S. missiles around the world could be launched against Communist nations. In 2001, the Cheyenne Mountain war room was closed, although it can be opened again in a matter of hours.

MINI-BIO

FLORENCE SABIN: FOR YOUR GOOD HEALTH

Florence Rena Sabin (1871–1953) was the first female full professor at Johns Hopkins Medical School in Baltimore, Maryland. In 1946, Sabin became the head of the Colorado State Committee on Health. Sabin demanded pasteurization of milk, sewage treatment plants, and public health education programs. In Denver, she began programs for diagnosing and treating tuberculosis and providing public health classes. She also worked to rid the city of disease-carrying rats.

Want to know more? Visit www.factsfornow.scholastic.com and enter the keyword **Colorado.**

CIVIL RIGHTS

Civil rights became a major issue in Colorado after World War II. Many African Americans and Latinos had fought in the war. Many suffered injuries or died. When these veterans returned to Colorado after the war, they

WORD TO KNOW

Communist *supporter of communism, a system of government in which all goods are held in common*

expected to be treated as equals, but weren't. They protested against **segregation** in their home state.

During the 1950s, the exclusively white Park Hill neighborhood of Denver changed dramatically. The community became racially mixed when African Americans and Latinos purchased homes and rented apartments in Park Hill. To overcome the racial tensions that arose, neighborhood ministers and concerned citizens formed the Park Hill Action Committee. The group's success was remarkable because it cost very little, yet produced racial harmony.

In Denver, African American and Latino students attended schools with few white students. In the lawsuit *Keyes v. Denver School District No. 1,* argued in 1973, the U.S. Supreme Court stated that schools could not be segregated. Denver public schools were ordered to desegregate.

WORD TO KNOW

segregation *separation from others, according to race, class, ethnic group, religion, or other factors*

SHIFT IN INDUSTRIES AND WORKFORCE

During the 1970s and 1980s, national concern for oil reserves and rising gasoline prices forced energy companies to investigate other sources for petroleum and coal. Oil shale (rocks with petroleum-like liquids that are released when heated) mining and coal mining brought jobs to western Colorado. Coal mining reached new production levels, but oil shale mining did not thrive. In 1982, the Exxon Corporation closed its oil shale mining sites in Mesa, Rio Blanco, and Garfield counties, putting thousands of people out of work. While mining opportunities fell, technology industries in Colorado were on the rise. The state became a major manufacturer of computer parts, instruments, aerospace materials, and electronics components.

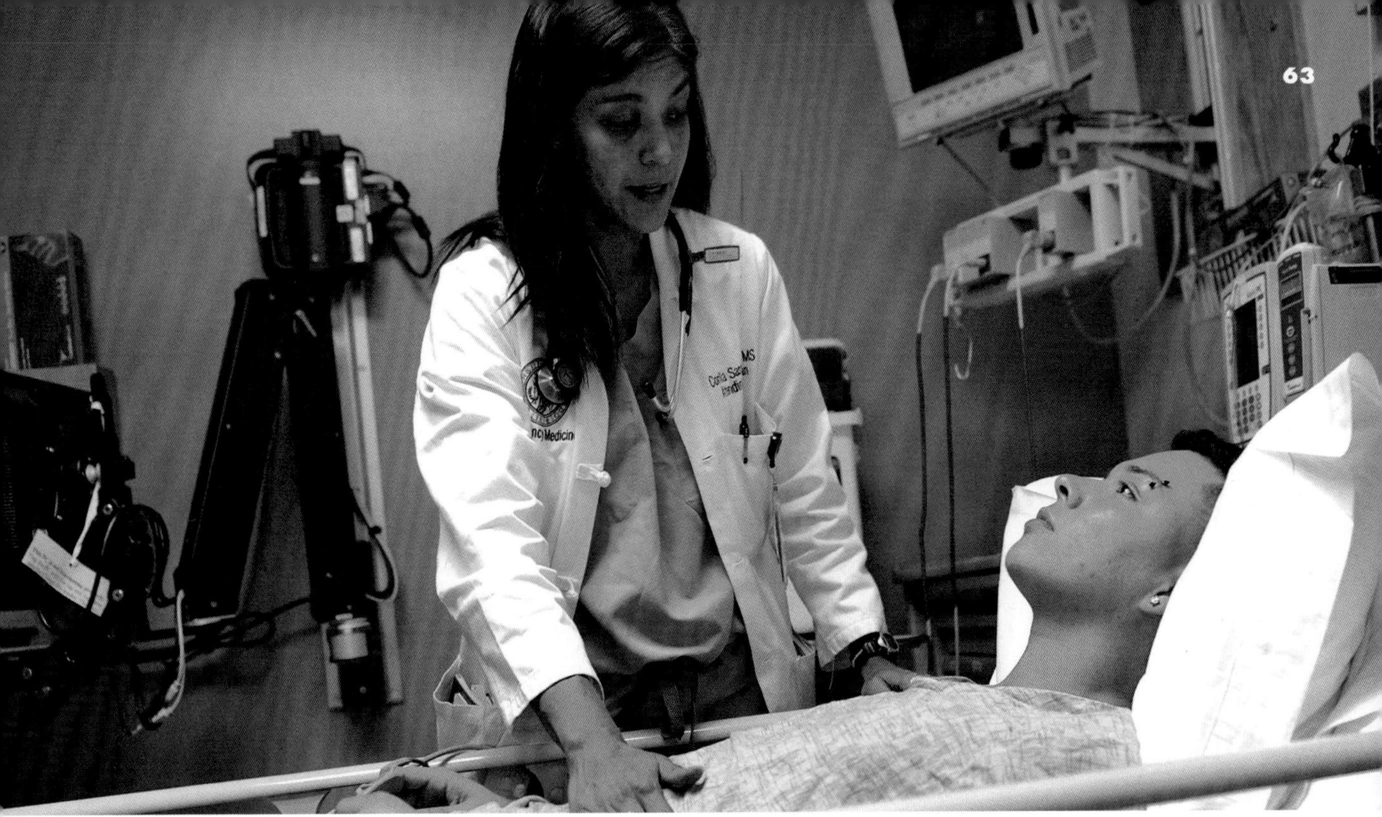

A doctor at the University of Colorado Hospital checks on a patient.

Along with a rise in high-tech industries, Colorado saw a marked increase in the numbers of women entering the workforce. Slightly more than half of Colorado's working women work in low-paying administrative, clerical, or unskilled jobs. This trend is slowly changing, as women make inroads into higher-paying management and executive positions.

By the early 1990s, Denver area drivers often faced traffic-jammed highways. The solution to this problem was expanding the highway system and building a light-rail, an electric railway that connects Denver suburbs with city centers. Begun in 1994, the Denver light rail system has 36 stations, and at more than half of them commuters can park for free and take a train into the city. The result is a cost-effective, quick means of transportation into the city. It is hoped that light-rail commuting will reduce the heavy air pollution in the Denver-Boulder region, particularly in the summer when pollution is at its worst.

A Denver light rail vehicle makes a stop on its 5-mile (8 km) route.

TRAGEDY AND ITS LEGACY

In the spring of 1999, tragedy struck Columbine High School, in Littleton, when two armed students went on a rampage, killing 12 fellow students and one teacher, and injuring 23 others. The event drew national concern and media attention and brought about a debate regarding school safety. Interest arose in finding ways to control access to guns, especially for minors.

A year later, dry conditions led to destructive wildfires in the state. The Bobcat Gulch fire near Fort Collins burned 10,600 acres (4,290 ha) of forest and destroyed 22 buildings. To the south, the Hi Meadow fire burned as much land and 42 buildings. In 2002, the Hayman Fire near Colorado Springs became the largest fire in state history at the time. More than 138,000 acres (55,800 ha) were lost. Wildfires burn away low-lying shrubs that hold topsoil in place and prevent erosion. Even after fires are contained, flooding and erosion damage during heavy rains remain threats.

A decade later, Coloradans faced eerily similar tragedies. In June 2012, after an extremely dry winter, a devastating series of wildfires broke out. The fires burned a total of 388,000 acres (157,000 ha), destroying more than 600 homes and taking the lives of six people. Then, just a month later, a young man with three guns entered a movie theater in Aurora and fired into the audience. Twelve people were killed and 58 were injured. The horrific incident, along with the December 2012 elementary school shootings in Newtown, Connecticut, again raised the issue of gun violence in the United States.

In spite of these tragedies, the people of Colorado are optimistic about the future. They are looking for ways to work together to prevent environmental crises, remain safe, and help their state grow. The state's economy is thriving. By the summer of 2013, its job growth had returned to the levels it enjoyed before the economy slumped in 2007–2009.

While the Black Forest fire near Colorado Springs in 2013 wasn't the largest wildfire in state history, it was the most destructive.

READ ABOUT

A street performer entertains a crowd in Boulder.

CHAPTER SIX

PEOPLE

★

COLORADO MIXES OLD WEST AND A RICH CULTURAL HERITAGE WITH A MODERN INTERNATIONAL FLAIR. Many Coloradans can trace their ancestors back to Mexican settlers, East Coast prospectors, Native American groups, or early Chinese immigrants. Later, Cambodian, Hmong, Laotian, and Vietnamese immigrants came from Southeast Asia to start new lives in Colorado after the Vietnam War. Each group has contributed to Colorado's rich cultural mix.

People QuickFacts

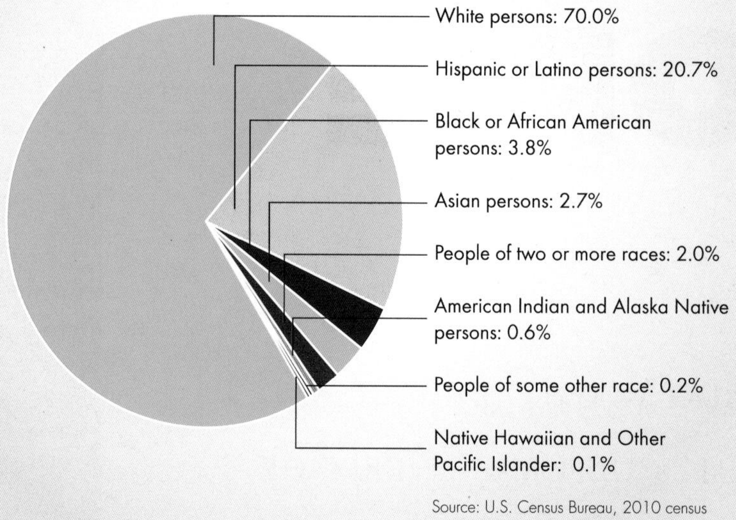

Source: U.S. Census Bureau, 2010 census

COLORADO DEMOGRAPHICS

A vast majority, 86 percent, of Coloradans live in urban areas. The rest live in small towns and villages or on farms. And more than one-third of all Coloradans live in cities just east of the Front Range, in Denver, Colorado Springs, Aurora, Lakewood, and Fort Collins.

According to the 2010 census, more than 20 percent of Colorado's citizens are of

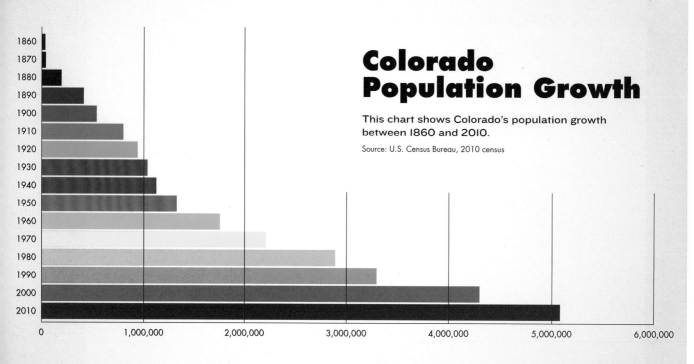

Colorado Population Growth

This chart shows Colorado's population growth between 1860 and 2010.

Source: U.S. Census Bureau, 2010 census

1860
1870
1880
1890
1900
1910
1920
1930
1940
1950
1960
1970
1980
1990
2000
2010

0 1,000,000 2,000,000 3,000,000 4,000,000 5,000,000 6,000,000

Hispanic or Latino origin. Many Hispanic Coloradans trace their roots to Mexico, others to the early New Mexico settlers of colonial Spanish origin. In fact, the 2010 Census reported that 11.8 percent of people in the state, age five and up, speak Spanish at home.

EDUCATION

Colorado's first school opened in 1860, the year of the gold rush. Three years later, tax funds began supporting elementary schools, and, eventually, public education expanded to cover preschool through college. In 2013, there were approximately 840,000 students attending Colorado's public schools. The number of schools changes regularly to keep up with the state's constant population growth.

Most public schools have a five-day week, but about one-third of Colorado's school districts have a four-day week, with school days lasting 7.5 hours rather than 6 hours. Some schools run all year long; others adjust their schedules to accommodate difficult winter travel or overcrowded conditions.

Colorado students and parents have a number of educational options to choose from. Parents, teachers, and community members can operate a charter school under the guidance of the school district. Charter schools address the needs of students and parents who may prefer an alternative to standard classroom education. Some charter schools allow students to work at their own pace in small classes. Several thousand Colorado students are homeschooled.

Many students take advantage of the 34 schools that deliver educational programs over the Internet. In the 2012–2013 school year, 17,289 students enrolled in Colorado online schools. Six of these online schools

Big City Life

This list shows the population of Colorado's biggest cities.

Denver	600,158
Colorado Springs	417,335
Aurora	325,078
Fort Collins	143,986
Lakewood	142,980

Source: U.S. Census Bureau, 2010 census

Where Coloradans Live

The colors on this map indicate population density throughout the state. The darker the color, the more people live there.

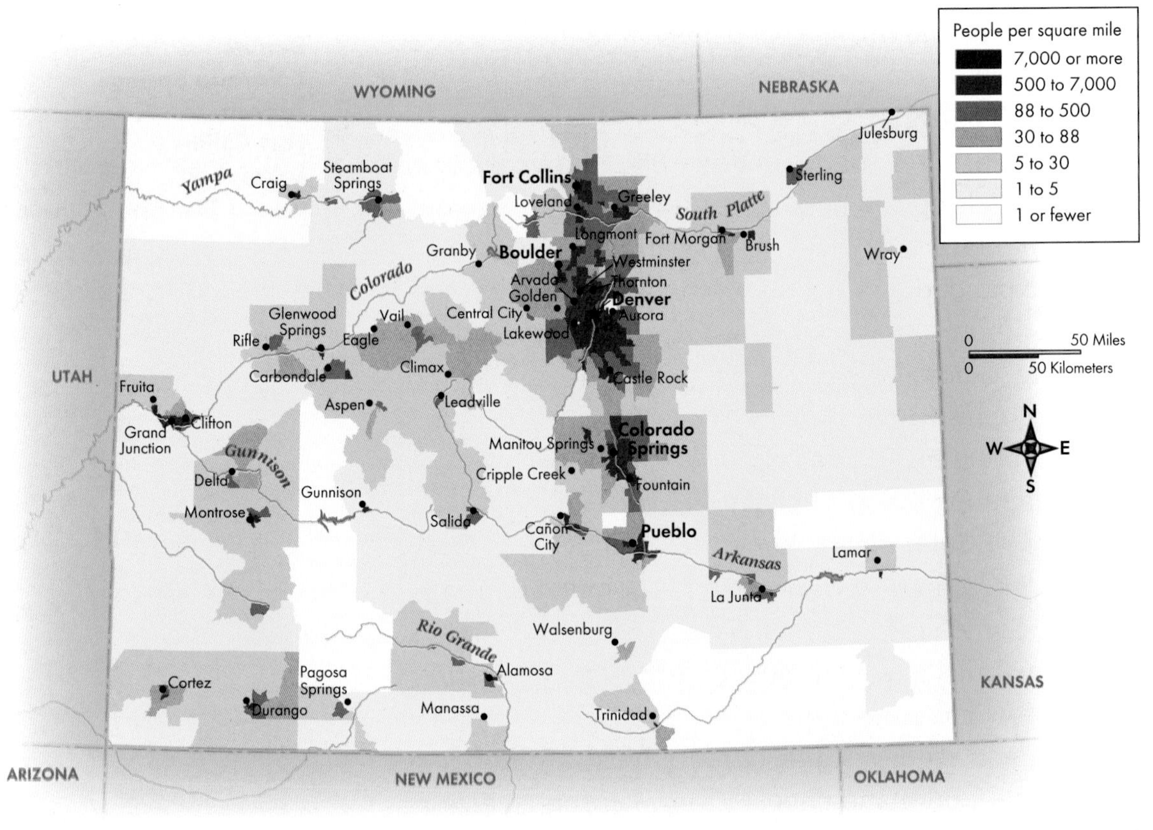

provide full-time programs, as well as additional courses. Students from ages 5 to 21 throughout the state take courses in math, science, social studies, and language. They are evaluated through assignments and projects. Colorado also has magnet or focus schools targeted at teaching math, science, art, music, or other specific subjects.

Colorado has 52 institutions of higher education. U.S. Air Force Academy students must be nominated

A student studying outside at the University of Colorado at Boulder

by one of their state's U.S. representatives to attend the school. This appointment is not strictly political but is instead based on a student's character, academic achievements, and activities. Colorado School of Mines, founded in 1874, is an elite geological/mining school with a worldwide reputation. The state's oldest college is the University of Denver, founded in 1864.

The University of Colorado at Boulder offers degrees in 150 subject areas. Scientists at the university's Laboratory for Atmospheric and Space Physics designed and built a special instrument for NASA's MESSENGER Mission, launched in 2004. The instrument measured atmospheric changes on Venus as the space vehicle flew past the planet in June 2007.

TALK LIKE A COWBOY . . .

boneyard cemetery
bronco untamed horse
buckaroo a cowhand that breaks wild horses
chuckwagon a wagon carrying food and cooking equipment
cowpuncher cowboy
dogie motherless calf or stray
greenhorn inexperienced easterner
hoosegow jail
hoss horse
lasso rope
maverick an unbranded range animal
pard partner, friend
range the open plains where cattle graze
windies tall tales

HOW TO TALK LIKE A COLORADAN

Many words particular to Colorado reflect the state's mountainous terrain, from slang related to snow sports to the capital's nickname.

bag a fourteener: climb one of Colorado's 54 mountains that are at least 14,000 feet (4,267 m) high
gorby: not a very good snowboarder
LoDo: the lower downtown section of Denver
Mile High City: Denver's nickname
champagne powder: high-grade skiing snow

HOW TO EAT LIKE A COLORADAN

Beans and chilies are common ingredients in Colorado fare. Considering the state's number of cattle ranches, it isn't hard to imagine why beef is found on many menus. Fruits and vegetables grown in the area, such as peaches, grapes, and potatoes, are also popular.

Chili peppers

MENU

WHAT'S ON THE MENU IN COLORADO?

Wild Game

The state's hunting and trapping heritage is evident in contemporary fare. Bison, elk, and venison, as well as game birds such as pheasant and quail, are found on menus throughout Colorado.

Fruit

Peaches, cherries, apricots, plums, and grapes grown on the Western Slope are delicious just-picked or as jams. In the southeast, melons, such as watermelon and cantaloupe grown in Rocky Ford, are favorites.

Beans

Beans are a key ingredient in chili. In fact, many chili recipes have no meat—just beans and vegetables. Coloradans make a classic chili with Anasazi beans, a deep reddish-purple bean with white splotches that was cultivated by early Native cultures. The oldest known chili recipe is nearly 2,000 years old and has been handed down through the Ute people.

Denver omelet

TRY THIS RECIPE

Denver Omelet

No one knows why this particular omelet is called a Denver omelet. There are no ingredients typical only of Colorado, but across the United States, this combination of ingredients is always referred to as a Denver omelet. Have an adult help you make this delicious recipe.

Ingredients:

Butter-flavored spray
½ cup diced ham
½ cup chopped onion
½ cup chopped red or green bell pepper
3 eggs
2 tablespoons water
½ tablespoon butter
Salt and pepper, to taste
½ cup salsa
Corn tortillas

Instructions:

Coat a frying pan lightly with butter-flavored spray. Heat to medium high. Add the ham, onion, and bell pepper and sauté until browned. Turn off heat and set the pan aside. In a small bowl, whisk together the eggs and 2 tablespoons water. Melt the butter in an omelet pan set to medium high. Pour in the eggs. Wait about 30 seconds for the bottom of the eggs to form a sort of crust. Lower the heat to medium low. Carefully stir the eggs with a fork, without breaking the crust, until the eggs set (about 3 to 5 minutes). Remove the pan from heat. Top the eggs with the ham mixture. Use a spatula to fold the edges of the omelet over the filling. Slide from the pan onto a plate. Add salt and pepper to taste. Serve with salsa and corn tortillas on the side.

Dancers perform in colorful dresses to celebrate Cinco de Mayo.

YIEMEI: COLORADO PAINTER

YieMei (1959–) was born in Taiwan, but she is a true Coloradan. She hikes, fishes, and skis, but her true love is capturing the scenic beauty of Colorado on canvas. YieMei's art includes florals, Rocky Mountain landscapes, and full-wall murals. Taiwan has a rich tradition of landscape painting that YieMei has brought to her new home.

Want to know more? Visit www.factsfornow.scholastic.com and enter the keyword **Colorado.**

VISUAL AND FOLK ARTS

Native American galleries throughout the state draw attention to the artistry and craftsmanship of the state's rich Indian heritage. Native artisans are known for fine beadwork, quillwork, pottery, weaving, and basketry. Sterling silver jewelry with embedded turquoise, quartz, and lapis lazuli stones represents a tradition of design and talent.

Colorado has stunning landscapes, and many of its artists translate nature's beauty onto the canvas as they paint. Alfred Wands is considered one of Colorado's best landscape artists, depicting many mountain vistas. Ken Elliott prefers the muted tones of pastels in his works featuring aspens in the autumn. Lakewood artist Greg Navratil paints nature studies that are so realistic, it looks as if the rushing streams might pour off the canvas.

LITERATURE

Storytelling is a Colorado tradition. For centuries, Colorado Native Americans sat around campfires and told the legends of their people. The tradition of storytelling continues at powwows and family gatherings. Later, cowboys on cattle drives sang songs, swapped tall tales, and recited original poetry. That tradition remains intact. The Colorado Cowboy Poetry Gathering takes place each January at the Arvada Center for the Performing Arts. This poetry is not just for men—cowgirls are also welcome to offer their verses about the role of women on the open range. Boulder hosts a festival of storytellers from around the state.

Colorado children's authors follow in a solid tradition of storytellers. Linda Hogan, a member of the Chickasaw tribe, is a poet, short-story writer, and essayist. Author Denise Vega keeps busy writing, speaking, and teaching. The author of *Click Here (To Find Out How I Survived Seventh Grade)* and other books, Vega visits schools, attends book fairs, and has worked on teen writing conferences. Young adult and children's author Julie Anne Peters writes for a wide range of ages. She is known for her Snob Squad series and *How Do You Spell Geek?*

Colorado's history of classic books is long and full. In the 1800s, Mark Twain traveled through the state and wrote of his adventures in the Rockies. Willa Cather wrote about Colorado's pioneering history, while Zane Grey and

MINI-BIO

LINDA HOGAN: CHICKASAW WRITER

Linda Hogan (1947–), a Chickasaw born in Denver, has become one of the most acclaimed and award-winning Native American writers. A poet, playwright, and author, she taught at the University of Colorado at Boulder. Her novel, *Mean Spirit*, which is set on a reservation in Oklahoma, gained a Pulitzer Prize nomination in 1991. She has also devoted her life to antinuclear, environmental, and peace movements, as well as to helping talented minorities and women advance.

Want to know more? Visit www.factsfornow.scholastic.com and enter the keyword **Colorado.**

Louis L'Amour brought Colorado cowboys to life in their novels.

Today, some 300 authors call Colorado home. Among the best known are Clive Cussler, author of adventure novels, and Diane Mott Davidson, who writes murder mysteries. Davidson's novels are set in Colorado, and her characters participate in many Colorado activities, such as snowboarding, skiing, and hockey.

MUSIC AND CITY STREETS

Music is as much a part of Colorado as snowcapped mountains. Opera Colorado

The Yampa Valley Boys play Western music with a banjo and a guitar.

brings the greatest hits of Italian composers Verdi and Donizetti to Denver audiences. The Colorado Symphony Orchestra fills the air of Denver's Boettcher Concert Hall with the sounds of Liszt, Mozart, Bach, and Beethoven.

While most dancers like to brag about how high they can leap, Boulder's Frequent Flyers take their leaping to extremes. These dancers work attached to lines from the theater ceiling, and twist, twirl, and jeté in midair.

With one in five Coloradans tracing heritages to Mexico or Spain, Latino art, music, and traditions are an integral part of Colorado's culture. Each year, Cinco de Mayo, the celebration of Mexican Independence Day, brings Mexican American dancers, singers, and citizens into the streets for parades and other festivities.

Mariachi bands feature five or more musicians, playing and singing Mexican songs. Mariachi bands are popular at weddings and street fairs, but one band is making a hit in the classroom. Mariachi San Luis goes into elementary schools and encourages students to learn about music history and techniques used in creating mariachi music.

LOCAL MEDIA

Denver is the media center of Colorado, with an abundance of television and radio stations broadcasting to Rocky Mountain residents. The *Denver Post* covers state and national news and is sold at newsstands throughout Colorado. Small towns have their own newspapers for local news. Some have rather entertaining names, such as the *Republican and Fairplay Flume* and the *Steamboat Pilot.*

Colorado's Hispanic citizens enjoy a variety of media in Spanish. Around a dozen radio stations broadcast in Spanish, and popular Spanish TV stations are available through cable or satellite dish. *Hispania News*, a magazine published in English and Spanish in Colorado Springs, is popular throughout the state.

THE GREAT OUTDOORS

Sports and outdoor life take up a great deal of free time in Colorado. The Denver Broncos football team were Super Bowl champions in 1998 and 1999. On the basketball court, the Denver Nuggets were formed in 1974. In hockey, the Colorado Avalanche has won the prestigious Stanley Cup twice, in the 1995–1996 and 2000–2001 seasons. When summer comes, fans pack the stands to watch the Colorado Rapids Major League Soccer team and the Rockies Major League Baseball team. In 2007, after an outstanding regular season and a National League pennant win, the Rockies made it to their first-ever World Series, where they lost to the Boston Red Sox.

Thanks to its many ski slopes, Colorado has been home to many famous skiers and snowboarders. Clint

The Denver Broncos play a game against the Kansas City Chiefs.

Snowboarder at Steamboat Springs

MINI-BIO

MISSY FRANKLIN: OLYMPIC GOLD!

At the 2012 London Olympics, 17-year-old Missy Franklin (1995–) competed in seven events—more than any other U.S. female swimmer ever! She returned home to Centennial, Colorado, with four gold medals, one bronze, and a world record in the 200-meter individual backstroke. After her success at the Olympics, Franklin decided not to turn professional, enrolling at the University of California at Berkeley instead.

Want to know more? Visit www.factsfornow.scholastic.com and enter the keyword **Colorado.**

Jones and Tommy Schwall are Olympic ski jumpers, both from Steamboat Springs. Travis Mayer and Michelle Roark participate in freestyle skiing, a sport in which skiers travel over **moguls** and do tricks in the air. Colorado's Courtney Zablocki takes part in luge—sliding down a winding track at great speed feetfirst on a narrow sled. Katie Uhlaender travels the same course in a sport called skeleton, going down the track headfirst on an equally narrow sled.

Many Coloradans would rather play than watch. Hiking, mountain climbing, hunting, and fishing attract avid athletes and enthusiasts across the state. When the snow falls, skiers and snowboarders put skis or snowboards on their car racks and head for the slopes. The people of Colorado enjoy good food and love spending time outdoors. They appreciate great music, beautiful crafts, and talented athletes. And they all know one thing: Colorado is a nice place to call home.

WORD TO KNOW

moguls *mounds of earth and snow that skiers move over*

READ ABOUT

Colorado students take a tour of the state capitol.

GOVERNMENT

★

THE CREATION AND IMPLEMENTATION OF COLORADO'S GOVERNMENT WAS A WHIRLWIND EVENT. In less than seven months during 1875–1876, Colorado's constitutional convention completed a final draft of a state constitution, it was ratified, and Colorado became a state. Its current government is still based on this original constitution.

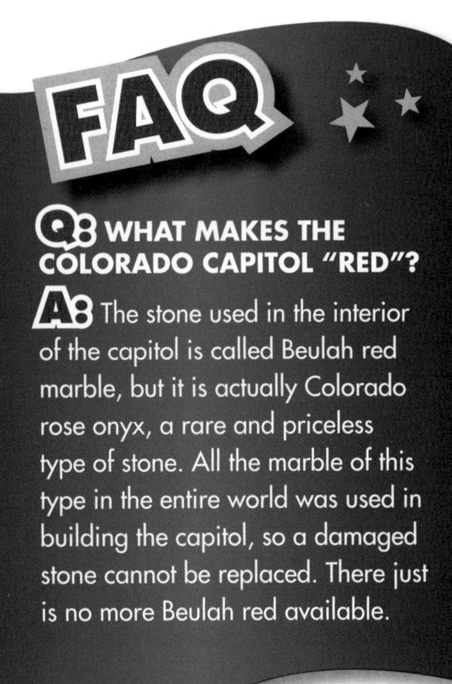

FAQ
Q8 WHAT MAKES THE COLORADO CAPITOL "RED"?
A8 The stone used in the interior of the capitol is called Beulah red marble, but it is actually Colorado rose onyx, a rare and priceless type of stone. All the marble of this type in the entire world was used in building the capitol, so a damaged stone cannot be replaced. There just is no more Beulah red available.

HOW THE GOVERNMENT WORKS

According to the constitution, the government of Colorado is set up in three branches: executive, legislative, and judicial. The governor, cabinet, and departments make up the executive branch. The legislature is comprised of the senate and house of representatives. The judicial branch includes the justices, judges, courts, prisons, and jails. The three branches work together to ensure the rights of Colorado's citizens. Denver is the state capital.

THE CAPITOL

Both houses of the Colorado government meet in the capitol. Senators and representatives have offices there. The business of making Colorado's laws takes place in the building's meeting rooms and offices.

The capitol is located in downtown Denver.

The capitol was finished in 1908 and was made with many Colorado materials. Only the brass and oak trimmings did not originate in Colorado. Stained glass windows commemorate the contributions of Coloradans in the past, and murals representing Colorado's history decorate the walls.

Capitol Facts

Here are some fascinating facts about Colorado's state capitol.

Built 1908
Elevation . . . . 1 mile (1.6 km) above sea level
Dome . . . . .200 ounces (5,670 grams) of pure gold leaf
Column. . . . . 122 cast-iron columns, weighing 1.7 tons each
Address . . . . 200 East Colfax Avenue
Architect. . . . . .Elijah E. Myers
Height . . . . 180 feet (55 m) from entrance to top of dome
Rotunda . . . . 128 pilasters, 60 spotlights, 16 stained glass windows
Mural artist . . . . Allen Tupper True

Capital City

This map shows places of interest in Denver, Colorado's capital city.

Q8 WHAT HAPPENS TO MONEY WHEN ITS OWNER CAN'T BE FOUND?

A8 When a Colorado official or business cannot find someone to whom it owes a tax refund, bank funds, wages, or any other money or property, the money or property is turned over to the state treasurer. It still belongs to the owner, who now must file a claim with the state to get it back. Since 1987, the Great Colorado Payback has returned $100 million in money and goods to current and former Coloradans.

GOVERNMENTAL CONCERNS

Colorado's government faces problems today in providing services and a clean, healthy environment for its people. Colorado has one of the fastest-growing populations in the United States. In 1950, Boulder was a small town with 20,000 residents; today, that population is estimated at 99,000 people. In recent years, the state's population has grown nearly twice as fast as the nation as a whole. Such population increases place greater demands on highways, housing, utilities, education, and other state services such as garbage collection.

THINK ABOUT IT!

Storing Water?

One of the biggest concerns for Colorado's government is ensuring that everyone in the state has enough water. This isn't easy to do—the population of the state is increasing rapidly, as it is in several nearby southwestern states that share surface water resources with Colorado. Some people want to recharge, or pump water back into, aquifers (underground pools of water) found throughout the state. As Denver water attorney Mike Shimmin says, "There's an impression that there's a vast potential for underground storage and all we have to do is rush out and do it. It's not that simple folks. It gets more complicated when you go to [a type of] aquifer where water doesn't stay put."

Among the issues state officials must consider are the quality of water being recharged into aquifers, the amount of energy needed to recharge the aquifers as well as to pump the water back out, and the location of the stored water relative to the people who need it.

Source: *Brighton Standard Blade*, October 4, 2007

John Hickenlooper signs the oath of office before being sworn in as governor on January 11, 2011.

THE EXECUTIVE BRANCH

The executive branch of the government is charged with the general running of the state. This includes education, state planning, the budget, energy management, and conservation.

The head of the executive branch is the governor. It is the governor's duty to enforce the laws of Colorado. According to law, Colorado governors serve four-year terms, with a limit of two consecutive terms. In other words, a governor can serve a total of eight years in a row, but cannot run again for a third term until another governor has served at least one term. State offices and boards advise the governor. One of the more interesting advisory groups is the Office of Policy and Initiatives. This office looks into every aspect of the state, helps the governor plan state policies, and works with the legislature to develop bills that address state needs.

Other elected offices in the executive branch include the lieutenant governor, the attorney general, and the state treasurer. The lieutenant governor is second in

SEE IT HERE!

GOVERNOR'S MANSION

Colorado's governor lives in the executive residence on 8th Avenue in Denver. A brick building with white trim, the house has spacious rooms for entertaining guests, as well as private family rooms. The crystal chandelier in the Drawing Room once lit rooms in the White House.

Colorado's State Government

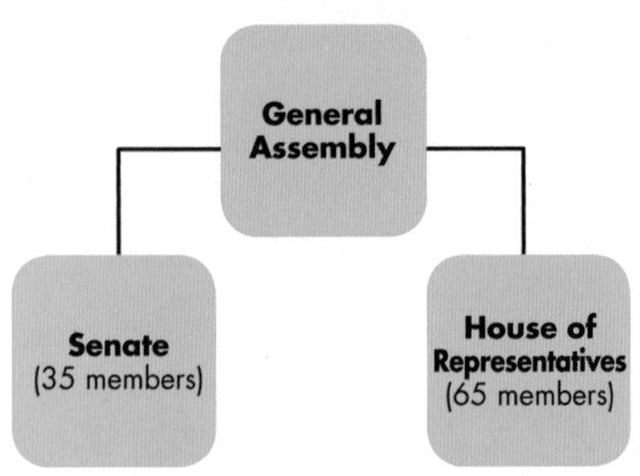

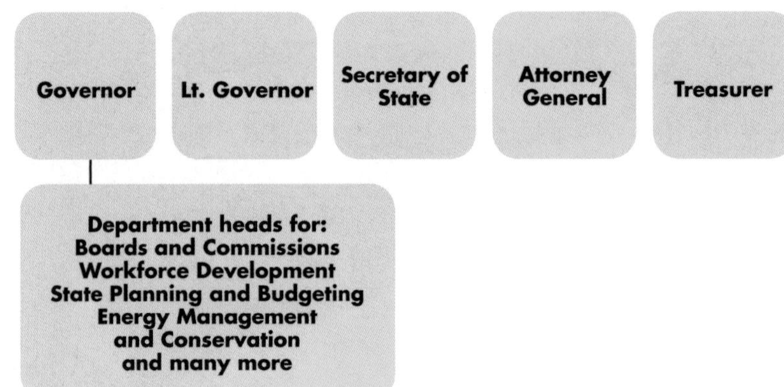

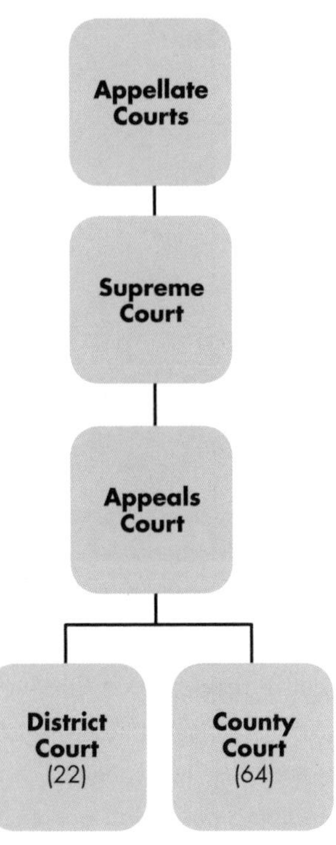

command and takes over for the governor in the event of serious illness, death, or crisis. The attorney general is the state's lawyer; through that office, criminals are tried and brought to justice. The treasurer serves as the guardian of all tax money collected and spent. The treasury manages a budget of $4.5 billion.

THE LEGISLATIVE BRANCH

The Colorado legislature is the General Assembly, made up of a senate and a house of representatives. The senate has 35 senators, and the house has 65 representatives. Members of the General Assembly are paid $2,500 monthly, or $30,000 per year.

The General Assembly proposes, investigates, and passes bills that may eventually become laws. Once the laws are passed, the governor must sign the bills into law. If the governor disapproves of a law, he or she has the right to veto it. The legislature can override the governor's veto by voting again and passing the law with a two-thirds majority vote.

Other states may allow their legislators to introduce dozens of bills each year, but not Colorado. Each senator and representative is limited to generating five bills a year, only two of which may be introduced during the month of December. This rule is to prevent lawmakers from crowding the legislature's schedule with last-minute bills before the year ends.

Senators represent people from specific areas of the state. They serve four-year terms and are only permitted to serve two terms in a row, a total of eight years. To make sure there are always experienced senators at work, elections are staggered so that only half the senate is running for election at any time.

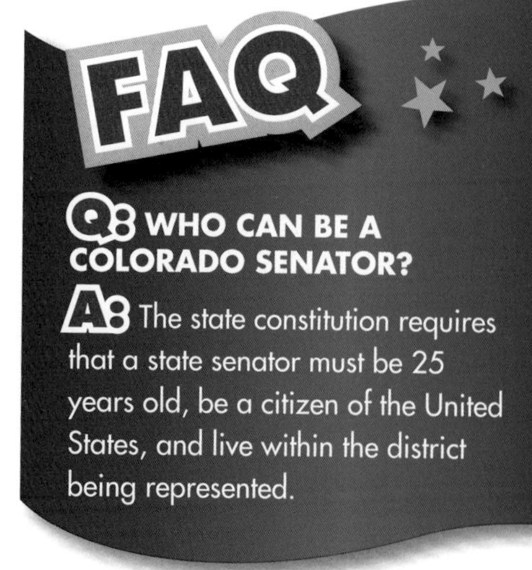

FAQ
Q8 WHO CAN BE A COLORADO SENATOR?
A8 The state constitution requires that a state senator must be 25 years old, be a citizen of the United States, and live within the district being represented.

Senator Randy Baumgardner (left) discusses a bill with Senator Ted Harvey (right).

Colorado Counties

This map shows the 64 counties in Colorado. Denver, the state capital, is indicated with a star.

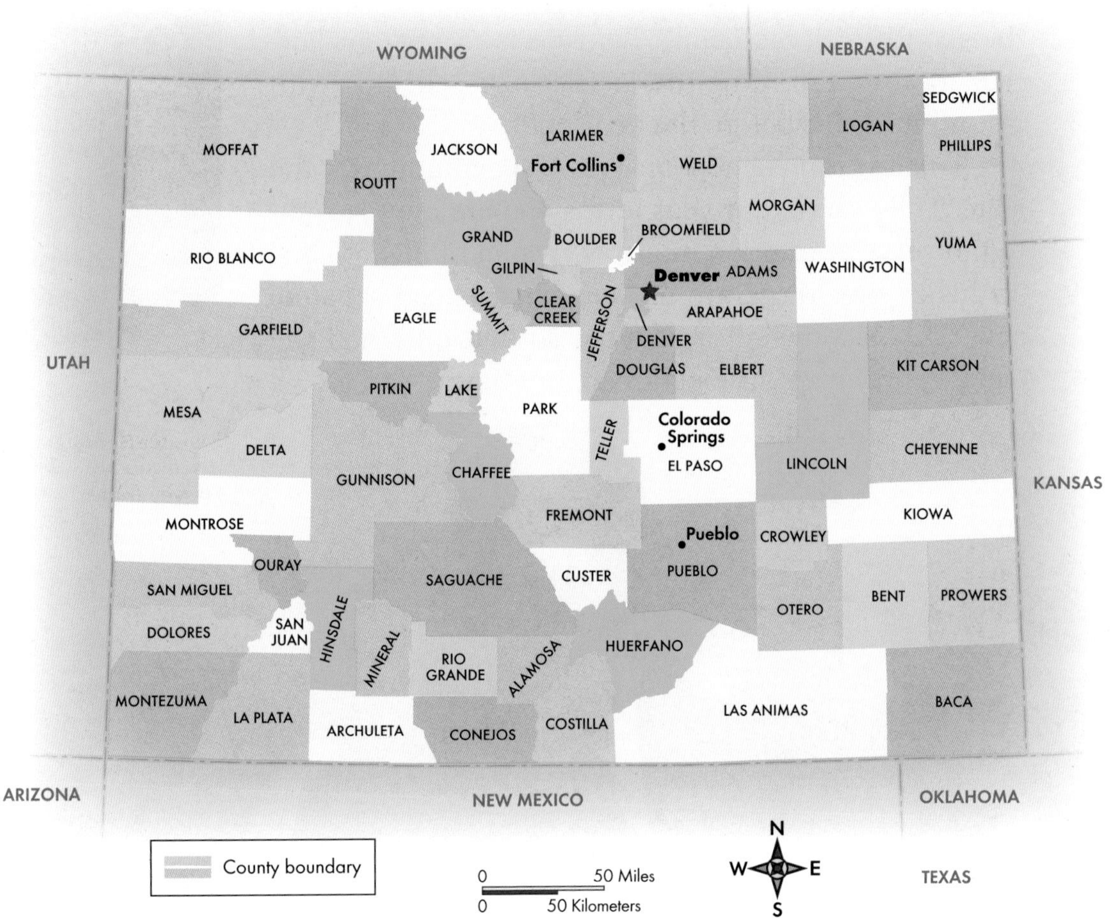

Members of the house of representatives represent a set number of people in a house area or district. While Denver has only five state senators, it has nine representatives, a number based on the city's population. Representatives serve two-year terms and then may run for reelection three more times, for a total of four terms and eight years in office.

THE JUDICIAL BRANCH

The judicial branch is made up of courts at various levels. The highest court is the Colorado Supreme Court, followed by the court of appeals, and district and county courts. The state court system has two main jobs: resolving disputes and supervising offenders who are on probation. Disputes may be crimes, such as murder or theft. In those cases, the state attorney general's office **prosecutes** a person or persons accused of committing a crime. Disputes may also be civil, such as a lawsuit, in which one person may be injured in some way by another and wants payment for damages.

The court system works in steps. Lower courts hear lesser crimes, and as a crime increases in importance or seriousness, the court hearing the case is higher in importance as well. In Colorado, when an opening for a judge occurs, a nominating committee interviews several potential judges and recommends two or three to the governor. The governor selects one and appoints that person to be judge.

The lowest courts in Colorado are municipal (city) courts, where judges hear cases such as those that involve traffic violations, shoplifting, and disturbing the peace. Each county has a court, and those courts handle traffic cases and civil or criminal cases that deal

MINI-BIO

BARNEY FORD: AFRICAN AMERICAN LEADER

Barney Ford (1822–1902), the son of an enslaved woman, escaped slavery in 1860 and headed to Colorado to take part in the gold rush. Gold mining did not prove successful, so he opened a restaurant and barbershop in Denver. He established literacy classes for African Americans. As a prosperous businessman, he actively opposed Colorado becoming a state unless African Americans were given the right to vote. Colorado honored Ford's contributions to the state with a stained glass window in the statehouse.

Want to know more? Visit www.factsfornow.scholastic.com and enter the keyword **Colorado.**

WORD TO KNOW

prosecutes *has someone tried in a court of law for a criminal or civil offense*

Judge Terry Ruckriegle listens to a case at the Eagle County Justice Center.

with less than $10,000 worth of goods. Only Denver has a slightly different court system, because it is both a city and a county. Denver's courts handle both municipal and county matters. A person would go to the Denver court for a parking violation or for robbing someone of less than $10,000.

District courts handle more serious cases, both criminal and civil. District judges are assigned to a judicial district and may hear cases in more than one district in the less-

WATER COURTS

Since its earliest days, Colorado has had water problems. Water rights were extremely important to ranchers and farmers in the 1800s and 1900s. If a rancher upriver built a dam and stopped water from flowing onto some other ranchers' lands, well, that was serious stuff. To resolve such problems, Colorado established water courts. There are seven water courts, one for each major river basin, and these courts hear disputes over water rights. The water court judge determines the verdict in a case. If one of the parties is not satisfied with the verdict, appeals are made directly to the state supreme court.

populated areas of the state. District courts may handle murder cases or other serious felony trials. They may also hear divorce cases, lawsuits for large amounts of money, and cases involving children.

The state has a court of appeals, located in Denver. This court has 16 judges and is organized in divisions, with three judges appointed to each division. The 16 judges include the chief judge, in charge of the entire court. Appeals are filed when the accused in a case thinks he or she has not received a fair trial according to the rules of law and the state constitution. The court listens to the appeal and decides whether or not the accused was treated fairly.

The last legal alternative in the state is the supreme court. If a person has made an appeal in the court of appeals and the appeal has been rejected, a final application can be made to the supreme court. This court decides if it will listen to the argument or refuse the appeal. The supreme court has seven justices and is led by the chief justice, who is elected by the others.

MINI-BIO

SENATOR BEN NIGHTHORSE CAMPBELL: A RENAISSANCE MAN

A member of the Cheyenne nation, Senator Ben Nighthorse Campbell (1933–) is a man of many talents. A jewelry designer, cattle rancher, and judo master, he served in the U.S. House of Representatives from 1987 to 1992 as a Democrat. He was elected to the U.S. Senate in 1992 and became the first Native American to serve in the Senate in more than 60 years. He wrote legislation for a National Museum of the American Indian to be added to the Smithsonian Institution. Campbell switched parties in 1995 and became a Republican. He did not run for reelection in 2004.

Want to know more? Visit www.factsfornow.scholastic.com and enter the keyword **Colorado.**

Representing Colorado

This list shows the number of elected officials who represent Colorado, both on the state and national levels.

OFFICE	NUMBER	LENGTH OF TERM
State senators	35	4 years
State representatives	65	2 years
U.S. senators	2	6 years
U.S. representatives	7	2 years
Presidential electors	9	—

TAXPAYER RELIEF

In the late 1980s and early 1990s, Colorado's expanding population put stress on existing public facilities. Colorado needed new schools in some areas and remodeling of older schools in the cities. A new convention center, an international airport, and a light-rail transportation system made Denver a highly desirable place for businesses to locate. The increase in facilities also meant that taxes would need to be increased to pay for them. But 1992 saw the passage of TABOR, the Taxpayers' Bill of Rights, which limited growth and spending by state and local governments.

TABOR allowed the state budget to grow based on only increased population plus the cost of living. Although this amendment to Colorado's constitution proved successful at first, and resulted in refunds to taxpayers, increased spending by state lawmakers created difficulties. In 2005, the government needed more money, so Colorado voters approved a suspension of the amendment for five years and then a capped increase each year. Some have questioned the legality of the law.

MINI-BIO

JOHN HICKENLOOPER: A GOVERNOR WITH A VISION

John Hickenlooper (1952–), born in Narberth, Pennsylvania, became the 42nd governor of Colorado in 2011. A geologist by training who later opened Colorado's first brewery-restaurant, Hickenlooper has lived in the state since 1981. He won his first race in 2003—for mayor of Denver. Although he campaigned for governor talking about budget reform and economic development, Hickenlooper has instead dealt with active wildfires and the issue of gun control. The year after the 2012 Aurora shootings, the Democratic governor signed several landmark laws restricting firearms.

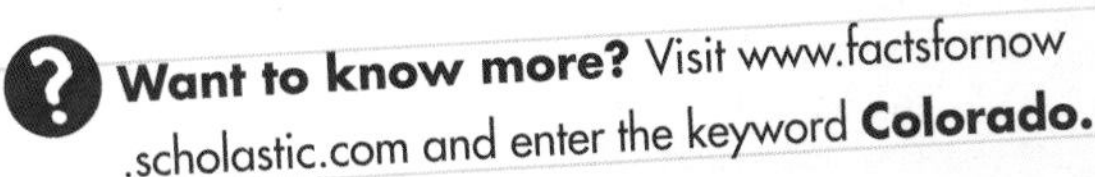

Want to know more? Visit www.factsfornow.scholastic.com and enter the keyword **Colorado.**

IT'S THE LAW

Colorado has a long list of laws that deal with children and their welfare. One area of great concern in Colorado is child labor. As a result, the government has passed a number of laws detailing the age at which children can work specific jobs. For example, a nine-year-old child can caddy on a golf course or deliver flyers. However, a child must be at least 12 to deliver newspapers, babysit, or work on a farm. At 14, children can work in convenience stores, restaurants, and at other nonhazardous jobs.

The court system takes care of children who are victims of crimes or who commit crimes. The courts will place a child in foster care or similar protection if a dangerous situation exists at home. For children who commit crimes, there is a juvenile court. Juvenile offenders stand trial in a different court from adults. A child found guilty of a crime may be sent to a youth offender facility, which is much like a strict boarding school.

Colorado's government faces many challenges at the beginning of the 21st century. The state wants to improve education quality, increase business opportunities, and solve its transportation problems. As Colorado looks to its future, it also seeks ways to conserve natural resources and preserve the natural beauty of the state's mountains, lakes, and plains.

State Flag

The Colorado state flag consists of three alternate stripes of equal width. The two outer stripes are a deep blue, and the inner stripe is white. A red "C" is slightly off center and to the left, in the middle of the flag. These colors represent environmental features of the state. The blue is sky, and the white represents snowcapped mountains. The red symbolizes the red soil of Colorado. Andrew Carlisle Johnson designed the flag in 1911. On February 28, 1929, the General Assembly stipulated the exact colors of the blue and red of the flag. The exact placement of the "C" was set by legislation signed on March 31, 1964.

State Seal

The circular Seal of the State of Colorado is an adaptation of the Territorial Seal, which was adopted by the First Territorial Assembly on November 6, 1861.

At the top of the state seal is the eye of God in a triangle with radiating golden rays. Below the eye is the Roman fasces, which is birch or elm rods (symbolizing strength) and a battle axe (symbolizing authority and leadership) bound together. It is the insignia of a republican form of government. Below the fasces is the heraldic shield. The top of the shield shows three snowcapped mountains and clouds in the sky. The lower half includes mining tools, a pick and a sledgehammer, crossed in front of a golden background. Below the shield are the words *Nil sine numine*, which is Latin for "nothing without the divine will." It is Colorado's motto.

READ ABOUT

Workers complete plastic smartphone cases.

ECONOMY

★

THE ECONOMY OF COLORADO BALANCES A TRADITIONAL STRENGTH IN AGRICULTURE AND MINING WITH THE NEWER DEMAND FOR HIGH-TECH PRODUCTS. From the time of the earliest settlers, cattle dominated the landscape. In 1858, the discovery of gold in Colorado created an interest in mining that expanded to both metals and nonmetals. Today, computer parts and communications technology are major industries in Colorado, along with mining and cattle raising.

Hotels are an important part of the state economy.

EARNING MONEY

Colorado's products are sold nationwide and internationally. Most exports go to Canada and Mexico, but Japan and South Korea also buy both manufactured goods and agricultural products.

Employment in Colorado has changed with the times. In the early days, farming and mining employed the most people. Manufacturing added to the employment base. Today, most Colorado employees provide services. They work in restaurants, hotels, motels, and at tourist sites. Retail and wholesale trades—the stores you shop in and the companies that supply those stores—also employ large numbers of workers. Other service workers include teachers, doctors, dentists, nurses, and bankers.

COLORADO INVENTORS AND SCIENTISTS

INVENTOR/SCIENTIST	INVENTION/DISCOVERY
Robert Seiwald	Antibody labeling agent
Aundrea Rosdal	Hotty Hoody, a cover for hot hairstyling tools
Rosario "Roy" Dolce	Two-handled putter
David Kubicka and Kegan Paisley	A rake for maintaining a smooth halfpipe at a ski resort
Tom Cech, John Hall, Carl Wieman, and Eric Cornell	Nobel Prize–winning physicists

Top Products

Agriculture	Corn, wheat, hay, sugar beets, barley, potatoes, apples, oats, peaches, pears, onions, sunflowers
Livestock	Cattle/calves, sheep/lambs, hogs, poultry
Manufacturing	Computer equipment and instruments, processed foods, aerospace products
Services	Hotel and motel, restaurant, health care
Mining	Sand, gravel, crushed stone, Portland cement, gold, helium, molybdenum, lead, zinc, copper

AGRICULTURE

Colorado has 36,100 farms. They range from small, family-owned farms to huge corporate-owned ranches. The average farm is about 864 acres (350 ha), though 54 percent of Colorado farms and ranches are less than 134 acres (54 ha). Colorado and cattle ranches go together. The big seller among Colorado agricultural products is beef, which amounts to $2.6 billion yearly. Ranchers also raise sheep and lambs, hogs, and dairy cattle. Dairy products and hogs (pork and pork products) are among the state's top five agricultural products. Some specialty ranches raise bison, elk, ostriches, llamas, goats, alpacas, or emus. Some of these animals provide meat for restaurants or gourmet markets (bison, elk, goats). Others provide hides (ostrich) or wool (llama, alpaca).

A cowboy uses his lasso in herding cattle into a corral.

EVERYDAY ITEMS

What are some of the ingredients from Colorado used in common household products?

PRODUCT	COLORADO INGREDIENT
Crayons	Wax
Paper	Wood pulp
Footballs	Pigskin
Shoes	Leather
Shaving cream, laundry detergent	Stearic acid, derived from animal fats

Grain crops, such as corn, wheat, hay, and oats, are the state's main farm crops. Farms also raise marketable crops of potatoes, sunflowers, peaches, grapes, and beans. Colorado agricultural products are also used in manufactured goods such as detergents, bandages, crayons, paper, footballs, shoes, and shaving cream.

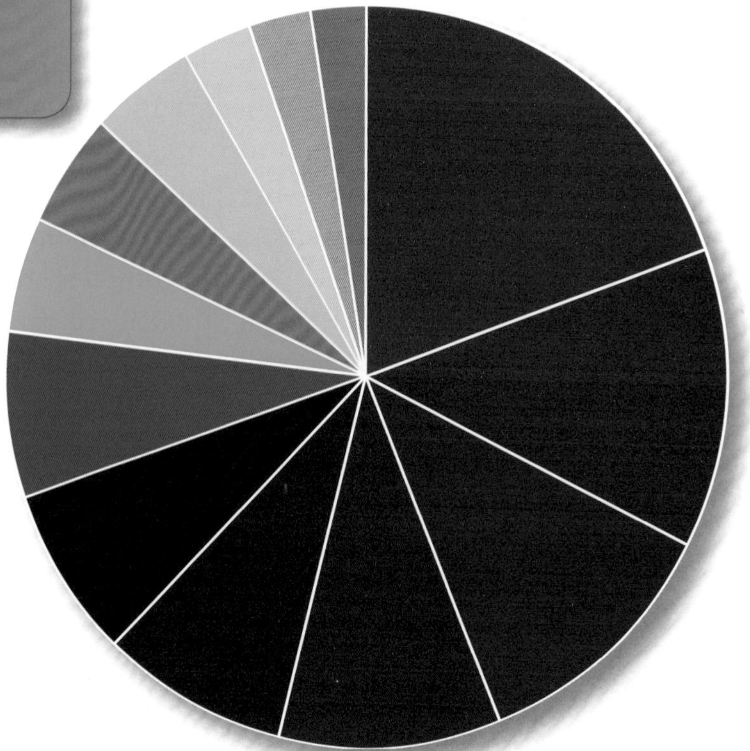

What Do Coloradans Do?

This color-coded chart shows what industries Coloradans work in.

- **19.6%** Educational services, and health care and social assistance, 484,269
- **13.0%** Professional, scientific, and management, and administrative and waste management services, 321,409
- **11.3%** Retail trade, 280,975
- **10.2%** Arts, entertainment, and recreation, and accommodation and food services, 251,748
- **8.3%** Construction, 206,174
- **7.4%** Finance and insurance, and real estate and rental and leasing, 182,815
- **7.2%** Manufacturing, 178,042
- **5.1%** Other services, except public administration, 125,972
- **4.8%** Public administration, 119,652
- **4.7%** Transportation and warehousing, and utilities, 117,321
- **3.2%** Information, 80,143
- **2.8%** Wholesale trade, 70,194
- **2.3%** Agriculture, forestry, fishing and hunting, and mining, 57,453

Source: U.S. Census Bureau, 2010 census

Major Agricultural and Mining Products

This map shows where Colorado's major agricultural and mining products come from. See a cow? That means cattle are found there.

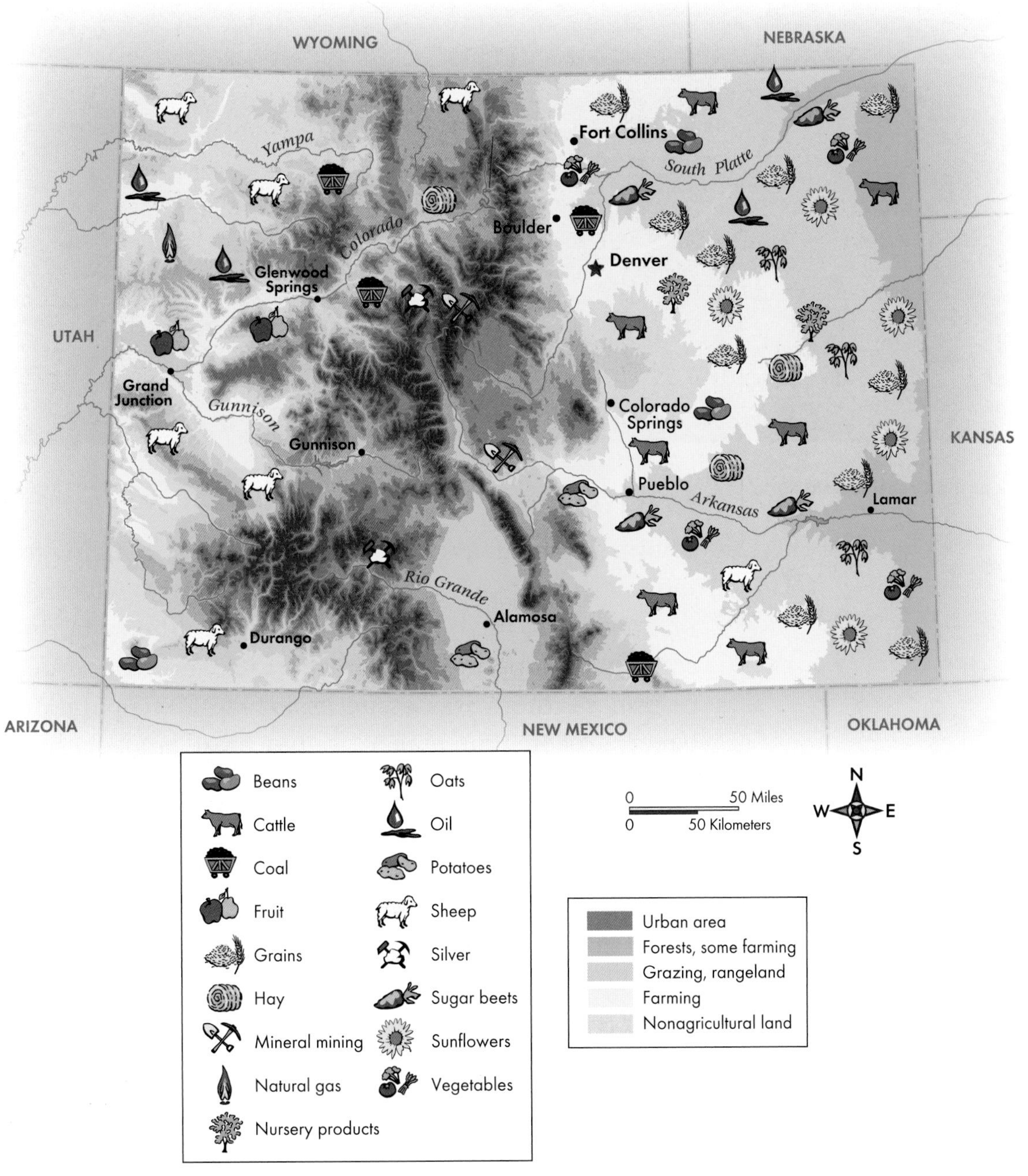

A dump truck at the Cresson Gold Mine in Victor

MINING

Mining has been a mainstay of Colorado's economy for more than 150 years. The 1858 discovery of gold drew prospectors to the mountains and many others offering services to support those prospectors. For every group of miners, there was a successful laundry operation, baker, grocer, tent maker, trading post, and clothier. Today, Colorado gold is used to make jewelry and in medicine and dentistry.

Gold is not the only metal mined in Colorado. The state has produced large quantities of silver, copper, and molybdenum. Copper, an electricity conductor, is used to make wire. It is also used, along with zinc, in making coins. Molybdenum provides strength to metal alloys. Colorado's titanium resource is the largest in the country and is used in making jet engines.

WOW

The Cresson Mine is the most productive gold mine in Colorado. In 2004, it produced 329,000 ounces (9,327,000 g) of gold. At today's prices, that is about $456 million worth of gold.

Nonmetal mining yields sand, gravel, and crushed stone for roads. Building stones quarried from limestone, marble, or granite are commonly used in the construction industry. The state also mines soda ash and sodium bicarbonate, both used in making glass. Natural gas, coal, and petroleum are **fossil fuels** mined in the state.

THE BUSINESS END

Ten percent of the **gross state product** comes from manufacturing, which employs more than 178,000 people. That is roughly 7 percent of all Colorado workers. Some workers process raw materials, yielding products such as vermiculite and paper. Others process food such as meat, handling and packaging it for sale in markets or restaurants. They can vegetables and grind grain into flour. Chemical companies produce adhesives and glues, beeswax products, dyes, and fireworks, among hundreds of other products. High-tech products include computing and electronics equipment and

WORDS TO KNOW

fossil fuels *products such as natural gas, oil, and coal that are produced naturally from decayed plants and animals*

gross state product *the economic output of a state, including all manufacturing, mining, and agricultural products, as well as services*

A worker packages tea at the Celestial Seasonings factory in Boulder.

A military commander keeps watch at the North American Aerospace Defense Command (NORAD) inside Cheyenne Mountain.

instruments. Two hundred aerospace companies produce engines and airplane parts and instruments for commercial airlines, military planes, and space purposes, along with guided missiles and satellite communications systems.

Finance, insurance, and real estate are major state moneymakers. Finance includes banking, investments, consulting, loans, and credit cards. Insurance provides protection for car owners, homeowners, and businesses. Health insurance covers medical, dental, and vision expenses, along with the costs of prescription drugs.

Tourism is big business in Colorado. Winter draws skiers, snowboarders, and snow bunnies—people who would rather be seen in the lodge than on the slopes.

Summer is a time to hike the mountains, fish the streams, and trek through the ruins of ancient cultures. Fall brings leaf peepers, tourists who head to the mountains to see the reds, golds, and tans of changing fall leaves. Whatever their reason for going to Colorado, tourists need services. They stay in hotels, motels, and bed-and-breakfasts, or they camp. They buy food in restaurants or grocery stores; they buy souvenirs, pay fees, and use local transportation. More than 100,000 Coloradans earn their livings by providing services to tourists.

As the population has continued to expand, so have the businesses and services that support it. Agriculture and manufacturing remain constant producers for the state, and high-tech and aerospace industries add to its economic health.

ARTS AND CRAFTS

The Native American Trading Company in Denver sells stunningly beautiful Native American arts and crafts. Indian chief's blankets and 19th-century Saltillo serapes (woven blankets worn as cloaks) line the walls alongside a colorful Navajo weaving. The gallery displays Native American jewelry, prayer feathers and fans, and unique pottery by skilled Native artists. The Trading Company is one of many art galleries selling authentic Native American arts and crafts in Colorado.

Skiers enjoy the winter season at the Copper Mountain resort.

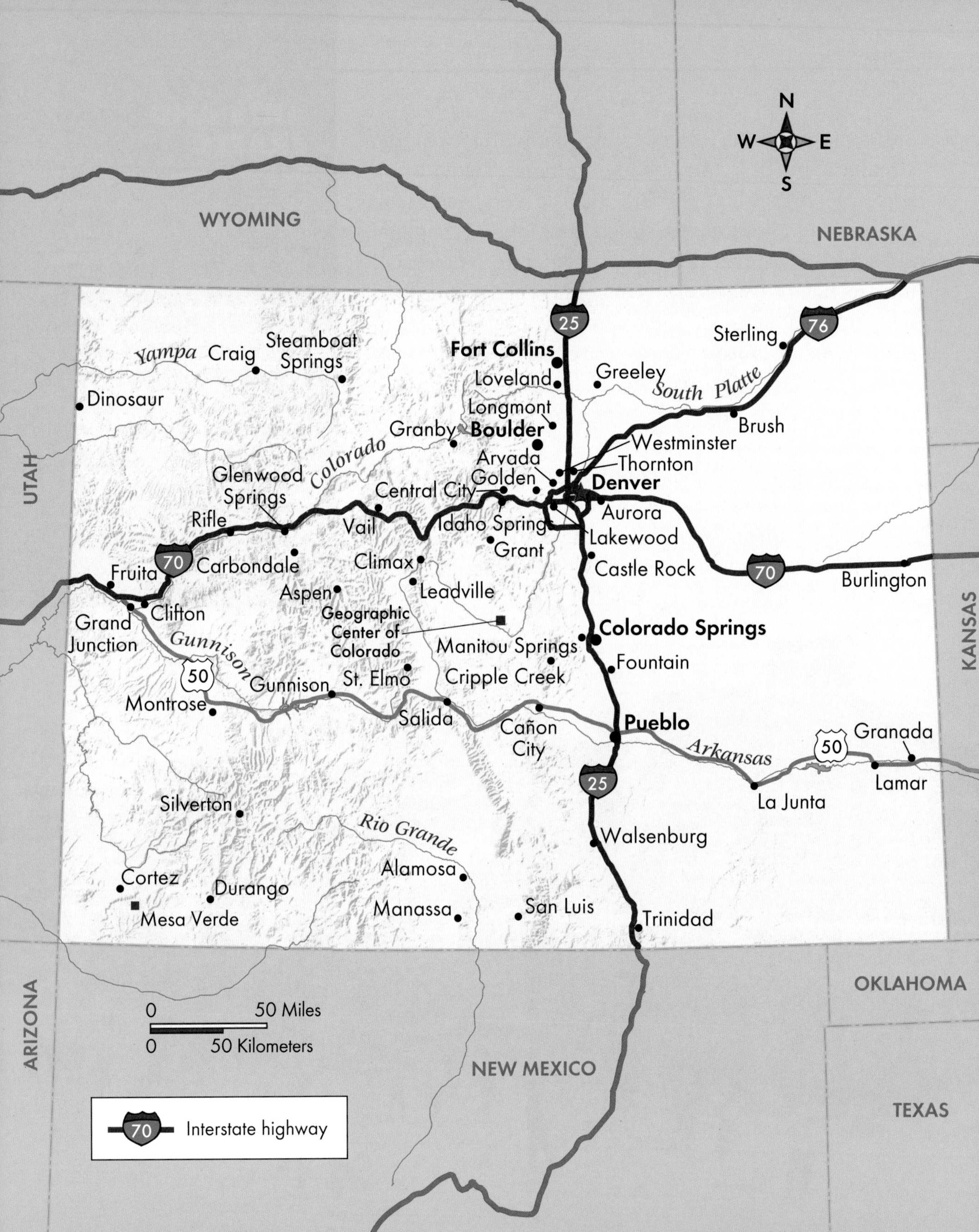
N
W
E
S
WYOMING
NEBRASKA
UTAH
KANSAS
ARIZONA
OKLAHOMA
NEW MEXICO
TEXAS
25
76
70
50
Yampa
Craig
Steamboat Springs
Dinosaur
Fort Collins
Loveland
Greeley
South Platte
Sterling
Longmont
Brush
Granby
Boulder
Westminster
Colorado
Arvada
Thornton
Glenwood Springs
Golden
Denver
Central City
Rifle
Vail
Idaho Springs
Aurora
Lakewood
Grant
Carbondale
Climax
Castle Rock
Fruita
Burlington
Aspen
Leadville
Clifton
Grand Junction
Geographic Center of Colorado
Colorado Springs
Gunnison
Manitou Springs
Fountain
Cripple Creek
Gunnison
St. Elmo
Montrose
Salida
Cañon City
Pueblo
Granada
Arkansas
Lamar
La Junta
Silverton
Rio Grande
Walsenburg
Alamosa
Cortez
Durango
Manassa
San Luis
Mesa Verde
Trinidad
0
50 Miles
0
50 Kilometers
Interstate highway

TRAVEL GUIDE

★

LET'S SEE COLORADO! Be prepared to climb peaks, cross gorges, and crawl up cliff sides. Start in the southeast and get a taste of the Old West. Then we'll snag some cutthroat trout from rushing streams on the eastern slopes. To the west, we'll investigate the Cliff Palace where the Ancient Puebloans lived. Next, it's north to the heart of the Rockies. Get ready—it's a wild trip over the mountains.

← Follow along with this travel map. We'll begin in Pueblo and travel all the way to Mesa Verde!

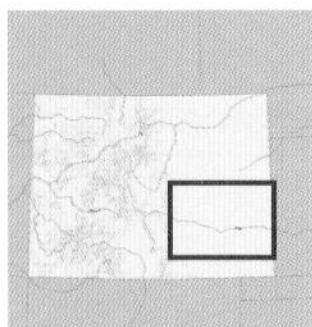

THE EASTERN PLAINS

THINGS TO DO: Go bird-watching in the Comanche National Grassland, take a walk among dinosaurs in Picketwire Canyon, or hop on a ride at the state fair.

Pueblo

★ **Sangre de Cristo Arts and Conference Center:** This site combines four art galleries, an IMAX theater, and a hands-on children's museum.

★ **The Colorado State Fair:** You won't want to miss this state fair! From homemade jams and pies to prized pigs, chickens, and cows, the fair shows Coloradans at their best. There are also concerts, exhibits, carnival rides, and great food—but it only happens in August and early September.

Along Route 50

★ **Big Timbers Museum:** This is for museumgoers interested in a bit of everything. You'll see guns and gowns, dolls and farm tools, and just about anything else you might find in great-grandma's attic.

Bent's Old Fort

★ **Bent's Old Fort National Historic Site:** In the 1830s, trappers brought their furs to Bent's Fort and traded them for cash and grub. Discover just how rugged their lives were at this historic fort.

★ **Koshare Indian Museum:** This cozy museum in La Junta has one of the largest collections of Native American artifacts in eastern Colorado.

★ **Picketwire Canyon:** Ideal for dinosaur lovers, Picketwire Canyon features more than 1,400 dinosaur tracks embedded in the rock.

★ **Comanche National Grassland:** The 440,000 acres (178,000 ha) of shortgrass prairie is the ideal place to see pronghorn, coyotes, black bears, bobcats, and 275 species of birds.

Prairie chicken at Comanche National Grassland

Colorado Springs and Surrounding Areas

★ **Seven Falls:** For sheer beauty, few sights can match the seven waterfalls that plunge into a red rock canyon at the foot of Cheyenne Mountain.

★ **Cheyenne Mountain Zoo:** Nestled on a hillside, the zoo showcases its elephants and giraffes in a natural African Rift Valley habitat.

★ **U.S. Olympic Training Center**: You might think that a sports training site in Colorado would only train for skiing and hockey, but the Olympic Training Center also trains fencers, gymnasts, volleyball players, swimmers, and others.

★ **Air Force Academy:** Founded in 1954, the Air Force Academy is one of the four U.S. military academies. Here you'll see the history of military aircraft.

Air Force Academy

★ **ProRodeo Hall of Fame:** If cattle roping and bronco busting interest you, you'll be thrilled to visit the ProRodeo Hall of Fame, where the best riders and ropers are honored.

★ **Florissant Fossil Beds National Monument:** Nearly 35 million years ago, volcanoes erupted and covered the redwood forest in this area. Today, lava and ash preserve the fossil remains of redwood trees, small plants, and insects.

★ **Pikes Peak:** Join the nearly 400,000 people who yearly travel up this fourteener in Colorado Springs. The climb is not nearly as difficult as it was in the days of Zebulon Pike. Today, you can take a small train to the peak. You can also ride your bike or drive all of the way to the top. Toward the summit, visitors get a view of alpine tundra with its low-growing shrubs and blue columbine.

★ **Royal Gorge:** Even the most spine-tingling roller coaster cannot compare with the aerial tram rides, steep railway trips, and walks across the suspension bridge at Royal Gorge.

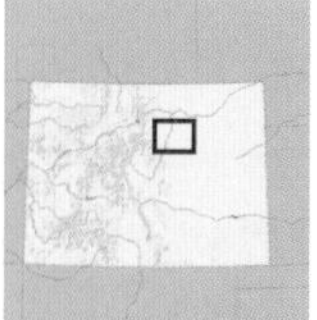

DENVER

THINGS TO DO: Visit the Black American West Museum, take time to smell the roses at the Botanic Gardens, or stroll through the trendy galleries of LoDo.

★ **Botanic Gardens:** This stop is a must for flower lovers. One of the top botanic gardens in North America, this site is home to 15,000 plant species, a conservatory, and 30 outdoor gardens, including one with flowers and water lilies inspired by Impressionist painter Claude Monet.

★ **Colorado State Capitol:** Visit the place where the state's lawmakers get down to work. The building is stunning, and the stained-glass portraits are vivid portrayals of the state's heroes.

WOW

The 15th step of Denver's state capitol is exactly 1 mile (1.6 km) above sea level.

State capitol dome

★ **Denver Art Museum:** All the best of Old West art by Remington, Catlin, and Russell mingle with 70,000 works by famous artists from around the world.

★ **Denver Museum of Nature and Science:** Learn about many topics, including the dinosaurs that roamed Colorado millions of years ago. This museum also houses the Gates Planetarium and an IMAX theater.

★ **Black American West Museum:** Dedicated to the African American cowboys of the Old West, this museum is chock-full of artifacts, clothing, photographs, and memorabilia from famous black cowboys such as James Beckwourth.

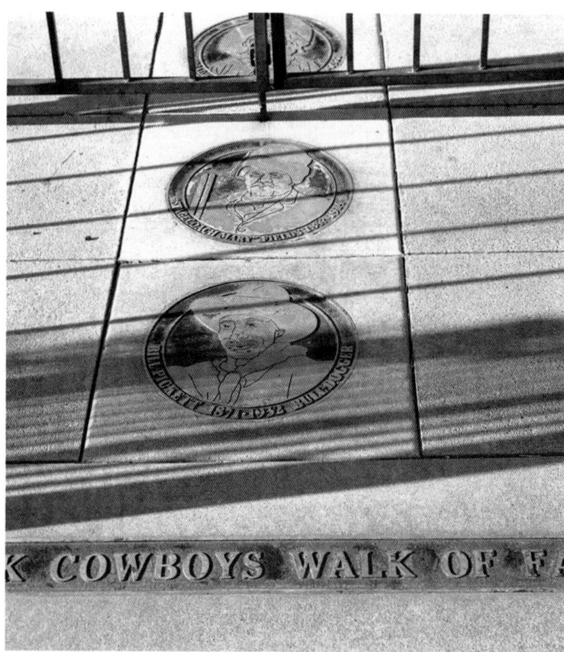

Walkway outside the Black American West Museum

The John Adams dollar coin from the U.S. Mint

★ **U.S. Mint:** If you think money grows on trees, you need to schedule a visit here, where coin presses churn out more than 7 billion coins a year.

★ **LoDo:** Take a walking tour of LoDo—lower downtown Denver. Enjoy art galleries, sidewalk cafés, statues, and shops.

★ **Wings Over the Rockies Air and Space Museum:** Climb into the cockpit of an old fighter plane at this museum, which is home to more than 48 historic planes and space vehicles.

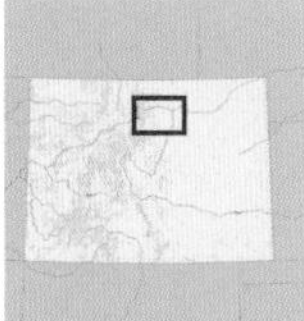

BOULDER AND SURROUNDING AREAS

THINGS TO DO: Trek the Indian Peaks Wilderness, stargaze at the Fiske Planetarium, or listen to street musicians on the Pearl Street Mall.

★ **Naropa University:** This is no ordinary college experience. Students go straight from chemistry class to tai chi, from advanced math to meditation. Naropa develops the minds, bodies, and karmic energies of its students.

★ **Indian Peaks Wilderness:** For stunning natural beauty, few places compare with Indian Peaks. This protected wilderness is right in Boulder's backyard and features more than 70 mountains and lush plant life. If you go in the winter, bring cross-country skis. There's a trail that takes you right through the park.

Indian Peaks Wilderness

Visitors at Fiske Planetarium

★ **Fiske Planetarium:** Regular programs take you to the stars, but the musical laser shows are truly out of this world. The planetarium provides several high-powered telescopes for patrons to use, and it offers classes on astronomical marvels such as quasars and black holes.

★ **Pearl Street Mall:** Meander through the shops, dine at an outdoor café, or enjoy sidewalk entertainment along this several-blocks-long outdoor mall.

★ **Dushanbe Teahouse:** The teahouse is a colorful tiled building based on similar structures in Central Asia. Settle down in the unusual atmosphere for an aromatic cup of tea and some delicious cakes.

★ **Boulder Farmers' Market:** Head to 13th Street between Canyon and Arapahoe on Wednesdays or Saturdays from spring through fall, and you'll get the freshest produce and tastiest jams and jellies around.

The Boulder Farmers' Market

The U.S. government owns more than one-third of the land in Colorado. That land is held in national parks, monuments, forests, wilderness preserves, and grazing areas for cattle.

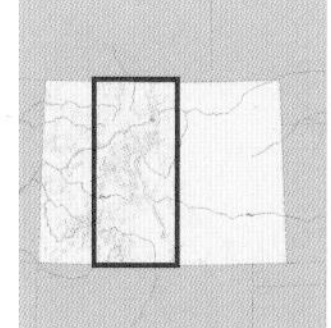

THE ROCKIES

THINGS TO DO: Ski at Aspen or Crested Butte, hike through Rocky Mountain National Park, or go whitewater rafting on the Cache la Poudre River.

★ **Skiing and snowboarding:** There are many ski resorts in the Rockies, stretching from Steamboat Springs in the north to Wolf Creek Ski Area in the south.

★ **Whitewater rafting:** When the snow melts each spring, the rivers run quickly through the mountains. Whether you speed down the Arkansas through Royal Gorge, the Cache la Poudre, the Yampa, or a dozen other rivers, this is an adventure you don't want to miss.

★ **Rocky Mountain National Park:** Trek past high peaks, cascading waterfalls, and bighorn sheep. If you are there in early spring, the crashes you'll hear are rams butting their heads together in hopes of winning the affections of local ewes.

Bighorn sheep

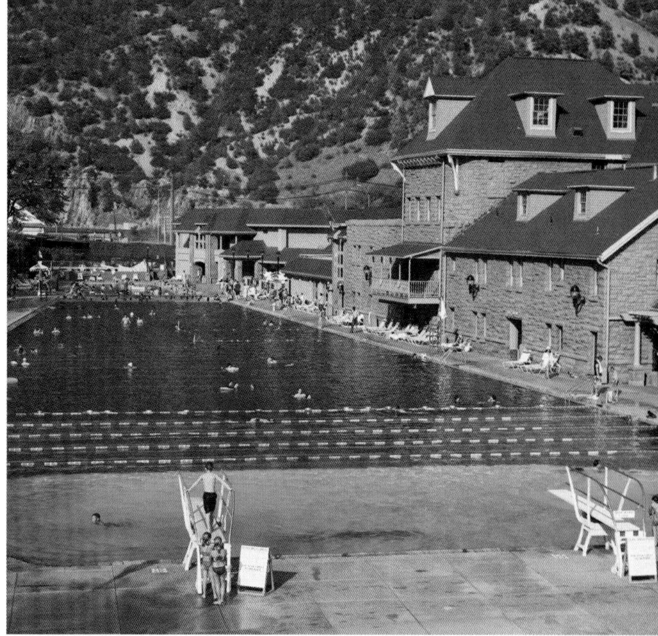

Glenwood Hot Springs

★ **Glenwood Hot Springs:** Soak in naturally heated mineral water. The pool is 405 feet (123 m) long and 100 feet (30 m) wide, and the water is always at just the right temperature. Two big slides provide enough splashing fun for the whole family.

★ **The Ute Indian Museum in Montrose:** This museum is dedicated to preserving the culture of area Native Americans and has exhibits about Ute history, arts, and way of life.

Great Sand Dunes National Park and Preserve

★ **Russell Gulch:** This former mining camp is on County Road 279—called Oh My Gawd Road. Hold on! This short 8-mile (13-km) road plummets down the side of a mountain and ends in Idaho Springs. It is a combination of hairpin turns, switchbacks, and steep grades.

The highest paved road in North America is the road to Mount Evans off of Interstate 70 from Idaho Springs. It reaches 14,264 feet (4,348 m) above sea level.

★ **Saint Elmo:** Here's a ghost town in the heart of gold rush country. The permanent population had plunged to 8 in 2000, down from 2,000 people in 1900. The town is nearly the same as it was 100 years ago, so enjoy a bit of history.

San Luis Valley

★ **Great Sand Dunes National Park and Preserve:** The highest sand dunes in the United States are not at a beach. Instead, they lie in Great Sand Dunes National Park and Preserve, where dunes cover 39 square miles (101 sq km) of land near the Sangre de Cristo Mountains. Plenty of wildlife and birds live here—bring binoculars.

★ **Alamosa National Wildlife Refuge:** This wetlands preserve is marshland in the floodplain of the Rio Grande. The refuge attracts songbirds, waterfowl, raptors, and some fabulous sandhill and whooping cranes.

Whooping crane

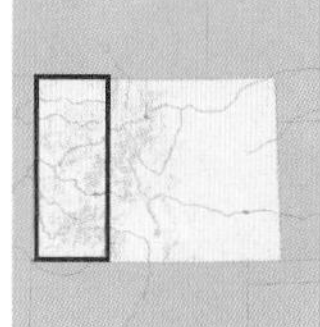

WESTERN COLORADO

THINGS TO DO: Visit a kiva at the Cliff Palace, step into history at Canyons of the Ancients National Monument, or investigate dinosaurs at Dinosaur National Monument.

Mesa Verde

★ **Mesa Verde National Park:** The Cliff Palace is the largest 12th-century cliff dwelling at Mesa Verde National Park. Built by hand, it has 150 rooms built into a stone cliff. Archaeologists believe that 100 to 120 people lived together in Cliff Palace at any one time.

Mesa Verde National Park

WOW

Four Corners National Monument near Mesa Verde is the only place in the United States where a person can stand in four states at once: Utah, Arizona, New Mexico, and Colorado.

★ **Canyons of the Ancients National Monument:** For people who enjoy ancient cultures, this is a must-see. There is an archaeological center, several active digs, and the history of a lost civilization.

Dinosaur

★ **Dinosaur National Monument:** This is one place where dinosaur bones still lie where they were found. Some 1,500 dinosaur bones remain embedded in a mountain.

Ute Mountain

★ **Ute Reservation:** Each spring, the Utes conduct their Bear Dance, which honors bears as sacred to the tribe. The Bear Dance is a line dance in which the Ute women get to choose their dancing partners, and the men are not allowed to refuse.

WRITING PROJECTS

Check out these ideas for creating campaign brochures writing you-are-there editorials, and researching explorers in the state.

118

ART PROJECTS

Create a great PowerPoint presentation, illustrate the state song, or learn about the state quarter and design your own.

119

TIMELINE

What happened when? This timeline highlights important events in the state's history—and shows what was happening throughout the United States at the same time.

122

GLOSSARY

Remember the Words to Know from the chapters in this book? They're all collected here.

125

FAST FACTS

Use this section to find fascinating facts about state symbols, land area and population statistics, weather, sports teams, and much more.

126

SCIENCE, TECHNOLOGY, ENGINEERING, & MATH PROJECTS

120

Make weather maps, graph population statistics, and research endangered species that live in the state.

PRIMARY VS. SECONDARY SOURCES

121

So what are primary and secondary sources? And what's the diff? This section explains all that and where you can find them.

BIOGRAPHICAL DICTIONARY

133

This at-a-glance guide highlights some of the state's most important and influential people. Visit this section and read about their contributions to the state, the country, and the world.

RESOURCES

Books and much more. Take a look at these additional sources for information about the state.

138

WRITING PROJECTS

Write a Memoir, Journal, or Editorial for Your School Newspaper!

Picture Yourself . . .

★ as a pioneer in Colorado. As the child of a miner hoping to strike it rich, you're expected to work in the mine, too. Or maybe your family received a land grant, and you've arrived in Colorado to establish a ranch.

SEE: Chapter Two, pages 24–31.

★ traveling with Spanish conquistadors. What would your days be like? And what people would you encounter?

SEE: Chapter Three, pages 32–41.

Compare and Contrast—When, Why, and How Did They Come?

Compare the migration and explorations of the first Native people and the first European explorers. Tell about:

★ When their migrations began
★ How they traveled
★ Why they migrated
★ Where their journeys began and ended
★ What they found when they arrived

SEE: Chapters Two and Three, pages 24–41.

Create an Election Brochure or Web Site!

Run for office! Throughout this book you've read about some of the issues that concern Colorado today.

★ As a candidate for governor of Colorado, create a campaign brochure or Web site.
★ Explain how you meet the qualifications to be governor of Colorado, and talk about the three or four major issues you'll focus on if you are elected.
★ Remember, you'll be responsible for Colorado's budget! How would you spend the taxpayers' money?

SEE: Chapter Seven, pages 80–93.

Zebulon Pike

ART PROJECTS

Create a PowerPoint Presentation or Visitors' Guide

Welcome to Colorado!

Colorado is a great place to visit and to live! In your PowerPoint presentation or brochure, highlight 10 to 15 of Colorado's amazing landmarks. Be sure to include:

★ a map of the state showing where these sites are located

★ photos, illustrations, Web links, natural history facts, geographic statistics, climate and weather info, and descriptions of plants and wildlife

SEE: Chapter Nine, pages 106–115.

Illustrate the Lyrics to the Colorado State Song

("Colorado's Flag")

Use markers, paints, photos, collage, colored pencils, or computer graphics to illustrate the lyrics to "Where the Columbines Grow," the state song. Turn your illustrations into a picture book, or scan them into a PowerPoint presentation and add music.

SEE: The lyrics to "Where the Columbines Grow" on page 128.

Research Colorado's State Quarter

From 1999 to 2008, the U.S. Mint introduced new quarters commemorating each of the 50 states in the order that they were admitted into the Union. Each state's quarter features a unique design on its reverse, or back.

GO TO: www.factsfornow.scholastic.com and enter the keyword **Colorado**. Look for the link to the Colorado quarter.

Research and write an essay explaining:

★ the significance of each image

★ who designed the quarter

★ who chose the final design

Design your own Colorado state quarter. What images would you choose for the reverse?

★ Make a poster showing the Colorado quarter and label each image

SCIENCE, TECHNOLOGY, ENGINEERING, & MATH PROJECTS

Graph Population Statistics!

Compare population statistics (such as ethnic background, birth, death, and literacy rates) in Colorado's counties or major cities. In your graph or chart, look at population density, and write sentences describing what the population statistics show; graph one set of population statistics, and write a paragraph explaining what the graphs reveal.

SEE: Chapter Six, pages 68–69.

Create a Weather Map of Colorado!

Use your knowledge of Colorado's geography to research and identify conditions that result in specific weather events. Create a weather map or poster that shows the weather patterns over the state. To accompany your map, explain the technology used to measure weather phenomena.

SEE: Chapter One, pages 15–17.

Gray wolf

Track Endangered Species

Using your knowledge of Colorado's wildlife, research what animals and plants are endangered or threatened. Find out what the state is doing to protect these species. Chart known populations of the animals and plants, and report on changes in certain geographic areas.

SEE: Chapter One, page 22.

PRIMARY VS. SECONDARY SOURCES

What's the Diff?

Your teacher may require at least one or two primary sources and one or two secondary sources for your assignment. So, what's the difference between the two?

★ **Primary sources are original.** You are reading the actual words of someone's diary, journal, letter, autobiography, or interview. Primary sources can also be photographs, maps, prints, cartoons, news/film footage, posters, first-person newspaper articles, drawings, musical scores, and recordings. By the way, when you conduct a survey, interview someone, shoot a video, or take photographs to include in a project, you are creating primary sources!

★ **Secondary sources are what you find in encyclopedias, textbooks, articles, biographies, and almanacs.** These are written by a person or group of people who tell about something that happened to someone else. Secondary sources also recount what another person said or did. This book is an example of a secondary source.

Now that you know what primary sources are—where can you find them?

★ **Your school or local library:** Check the library catalog for collections of original writings, government documents, musical scores, and so on. Some of this material may be stored on microfilm.

★ **Historical societies:** These organizations keep historical documents, photographs, and other materials. Staff members can help you find what you are looking for. History museums are also great places to see primary sources firsthand.

★ **The Internet:** There are lots of sites that have primary sources you can download and use in a project or assignment.

TIMELINE

★ ★ ★

U.S. Events **600** **Colorado Events**

600–1300
Ancient Puebloans build a cliff city at Mesa Verde.

1400

1492
Christopher Columbus and his crew sight land in the Caribbean Sea.

1500

1500
Utes inhabit the western part of Colorado.

1540
Francisco Vásquez de Coronado begins exploring the Southwest.

1600

1607
The first permanent English settlement is established in North America at Jamestown.

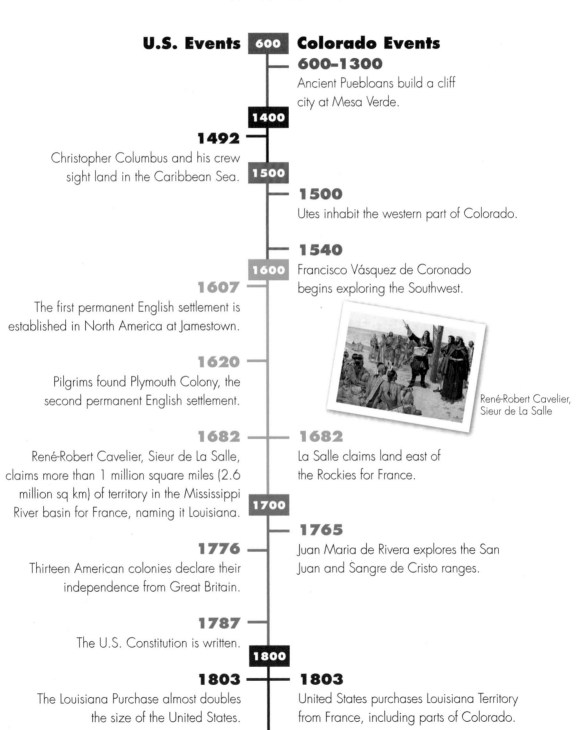

1620
Pilgrims found Plymouth Colony, the second permanent English settlement.

René-Robert Cavelier, Sieur de La Salle

1682
René-Robert Cavelier, Sieur de La Salle, claims more than 1 million square miles (2.6 million sq km) of territory in the Mississippi River basin for France, naming it Louisiana.

1682
La Salle claims land east of the Rockies for France.

1700

1765
Juan Maria de Rivera explores the San Juan and Sangre de Cristo ranges.

1776
Thirteen American colonies declare their independence from Great Britain.

1787
The U.S. Constitution is written.

1800

1803
The Louisiana Purchase almost doubles the size of the United States.

1803
United States purchases Louisiana Territory from France, including parts of Colorado.

U.S. Events	Colorado Events
	1806 Zebulon Pike explores the Colorado region.
1812–15 The United States and Great Britain fight the War of 1812.	
1830 The Indian Removal Act forces eastern Native American groups to relocate west of the Mississippi River.	
	1833 Bent's Fort serves as a trading post in Colorado; Mexican settlers receive land grants in Colorado.
1846–48 The United States fights a war with Mexico over western territories in the Mexican War.	
	1851 A settlement is founded at Conejos by six Hispanic families.
	1858 Gold is found along the South Platte River.
1861–65 The American Civil War is fought between the Northern Union and the Southern Confederacy; it ends with the surrender of the Confederate army, led by General Robert E. Lee.	**1861** Colorado is established as a separate territory; Civil War begins.
	1864 The army slaughters Indian men, women, and children at Sand Creek.
1866 The U.S. Congress approves the Fourteenth Amendment to the U.S. Constitution, granting citizenship to African Americans.	
	1867 The Treaty of Medicine Lodge takes Cheyenne and Arapaho land and moves those tribes to Oklahoma's Indian Territory.
	1876 Colorado becomes a state.
1886 Apache leader Geronimo surrenders to the U.S. Army, ending the last major Native American rebellion against the expansion of the United States into the West.	
	1893 Colorado grants women the right to vote.
1898 The United States gains control of Cuba, Puerto Rico, the Philippines, and Guam after defeating Spain in the Spanish-American War.	

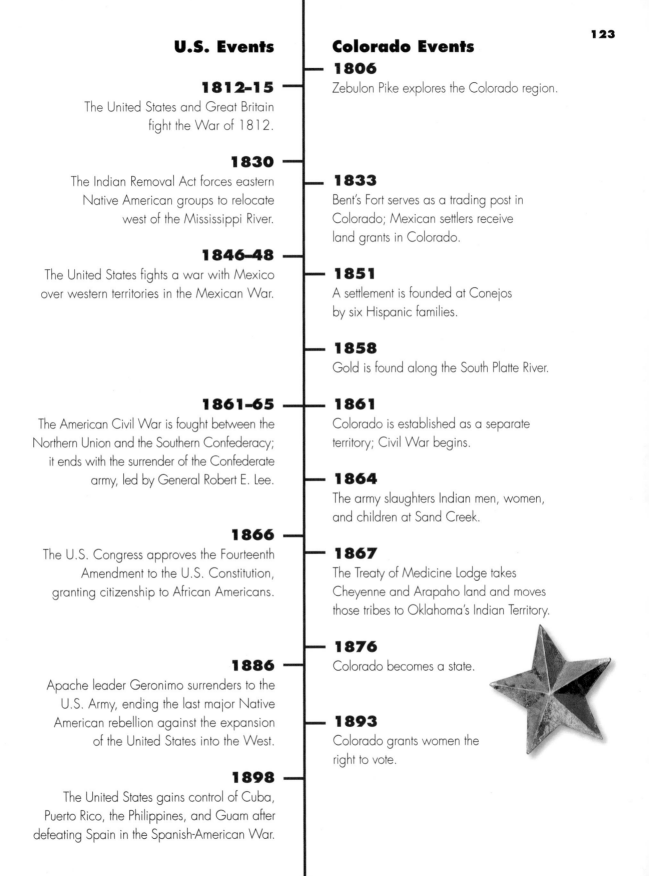

U.S. Events

1900

1917–18
The United States engages in World War I.

1929
The stock market crashes, plunging the United States more deeply into the Great Depression.

1941–45
The United States engages in World War II.

1950–53
The United States engages in the Korean War.

1954
The U.S. Supreme Court prohibits segregation of public schools in the *Brown v. Board of Education* ruling.

1964–73
The United States engages in the Vietnam War.

1991
The United States and other nations engage in the brief Persian Gulf War against Iraq.

2000

2001
Terrorists hijack four U.S. aircraft and crash them into the World Trade Center in New York City, the Pentagon in Arlington, Virginia, and a Pennsylvania field, killing thousands.

2003
The United States and coalition forces invade Iraq.

Colorado Events

1918
World War I increases the demand for molybdenum, mined in Colorado.

1931
Colorado's population reaches more than one million people.

1942
The federal government establishes a Japanese American internment camp named Amache.

1950s–1960s
Tourism industry flourishes, and the ski industry begins.

U.S. Air Force Academy

1958
U.S. Air Force Academy is built in Colorado Springs.

1973
Denver schools are ordered to desegregate.

1982
Oil shale mining stops on the western slope.

1999
Columbine High School massacre occurs.

2002
Hayman Fire, near Colorado Springs, is the largest wildfire in the state's history.

2012
Shootings at a movie theater in Aurora help ignite a national debate over gun control.

GLOSSARY

communism a system of government in which all goods are held in common

conquistador one who conquers; specifically a leader in the Spanish conquest of the Americas

conservation the act of saving or preserving something, such as a natural resource, plant, or animal species

depression a long period during which productivity is low, many people are out of work, and the value of money is unstable

erosion the gradual wearing away of rock or soil by physical breakdown, chemical solution, or water

fossil fuels products such as natural gas, oil, and coal that are produced naturally from decayed plants and animals

gross state product the economic output of a state, including all manufacturing, mining, and agricultural products, as well as services

headwaters the streams that make up the beginnings of a river

inflation an increase in the supply of currency or credit relative to the amount of goods or services available, resulting in higher prices

moguls mounds of earth and snow that skiers move over

pesticides any chemicals or biological agents used to kill plant or animal pests

prosecutes has someone tried in a court of law for a criminal or civil offense

reservation land set aside for a group to live on, usually Native Americans

segregation separation from others, according to race, class, ethnic group, religion, or other factors

sinew an inflexible cord or band of connective tissue that joins muscle to bone

spelling school similar to a spelling bee, with the added benefit of learning how to use new vocabulary

suffragists people who worked to achieve voting and other civil rights for women

telegraph a means of communication through which messages were sent along wires using a code of long and short (dashes and dots) pulses

watersheds land areas that drain water from a particular region

FAST FACTS

★ ★ ★

State Symbols

Statehood date	August 1, 1876, the 38th state
Origin of state name	From a Spanish word meaning "reddish," first used to describe the Colorado River
State capital	Denver
State nickname	Centennial State
State motto	"*Nil Sine Numine*" ("Nothing without the Deity")
State bird	Lark bunting
State flower	White and lavender columbine
State fish	Greenback cutthroat trout
State mineral	Rhodochrosite
State gem	Aquamarine
State insect	Hairstreak butterfly
State song	"Where the Columbines Grow"
State tree	Blue spruce
State animal	Rocky Mountain bighorn sheep
State folk dance	Square dance
State fossil	Stegosaurus
State grass	Blue grama grass
State fair	Pueblo (August)

State seal

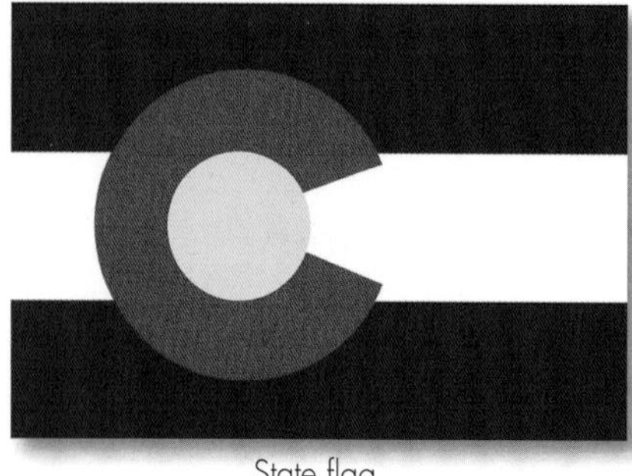

State flag

Geography

Total area; rank	104,094 square miles (269,603 sq km); 8th
Land; rank	103,718 square miles (268,630 sq km); 8th
Water; rank	376 square miles (974 sq km); 46th
Inland water; rank	376 square miles (974 sq km); 40th
Geographic center	Park County, 30 miles (48 km) northwest of Pikes Peak
Latitude	37° N to 41° N
Longitude	102° W to 109° W
Highest point	Mount Elbert, 14,440 feet (4,401 m)
Lowest point	Arikaree River, 3,315 feet (1,010 m)
Largest city	Denver
Number of counties	64
Longest river	Colorado

Population

Population; rank (2010 census): 5,029,196; 22nd
Density (2010 census): 48.5 persons per square mile (19 per sq km)
Population distribution (2010 census): 86% urban, 14% rural
Ethnic distribution (2010 census): White persons: 70.0%
Black persons: 3.8%
Asian persons: 2.7%
American Indian and Alaska Native persons: 0.6%
Native Hawaiian and Other Pacific Islander persons: 0.1%
People of two or more races: 2.0%
Hispanic or Latino persons: 20.7%
People of some other race: 0.2%.

Record high temperature 114°F (46°C) at Las Animas on July 1, 1933, and at Sedgewick on July 11, 1954
Record low temperature –61°F (–52°C) at Maybell in Moffat County on February 1, 1985
Average July temperature, Burlington 74°F (23°C)
Average July temperature, Leadville 55°F (13°C)
Average January temperature, Burlington 28°F (–2°C)
Average January temperature, Leadville 18°F (–8°C)
Average annual precipitation, state 15 inches (38.1 cm)

STATE SONG

"Where the Columbines Grow"

Words and music by A. J. Flynn

"Where the Columbines Grow" was adopted as the official state song on May 8, 1915, by an act of the General Assembly. The words were written and the music composed by A. J. Flynn. Traveling by horse and wagon to visit Indian tribes in the San Luis Valley in 1896, Flynn was inspired to write the song after he came across a Colorado mountain meadow covered with columbines. He dedicated the song to the Colorado pioneers.

Where the snowy peaks gleam in the
moonlight,
Above the dark forests of pine,
And the wild foaming waters dash onward
Towards land where the tropic stars shine;

Where the scream of the bold mountain
eagle,
Responds to the notes of the dove,
Is the purple robed West, the land that is
best,
The pioneer land that we love.

Chorus:
'Tis the land where the columbines grow,
Over-looking the plains far below,
While the cool summer breeze in the
evergreen trees
Softly sings where the columbines grow.

The bison is gone from the upland,
The deer from the canyon has fled,
The home of the wolf is deserted,
The antelope moans for his dead,

The war shoop re-echoes no longer
The Indian's only a name,
And the nymphs of the grove in their
loneliness rove,
But the columbine blooms just the same.
(Chorus)
Let the violet brighten the brookside,
In sunlight of earlier spring,
Let the clover bedeck the green meadow,
In days when the orioles sing,

Let the goldenrod herald the autumn,
But under the midsummer sky,
In its fair Western home, may the columbine
bloom
Till our great mountain rivers run dry.
(Chorus)

NATURAL AREAS AND HISTORIC SITES

National Parks

Mesa Verde National Park contains pre-Columbian cliff dwellings and other relics of early Native people; *Rocky Mountain National Park* sits along the Continental Divide and offers visitors panoramic views of the Rocky Mountains; *Black Canyon of the Gunnison National Park* is a sheer-walled canyon; and *Great Sand Dunes National Park and Preserve* contains some of the largest and tallest sand dunes in the United States.

National Historic Sites

Bent's Old Fort National Historic Site preserves a frontier trading post and *Sand Creek Massacre National Historic Site* honors and pays respect to the Cheyenne and Arapaho people.

National Historic Trails

California National Historic Trail, The Old Spanish Trail, The Pony Express Trail, and *The Santa Fe National Historic Trail* all passed through Colorado and are preserved for visitors.

National Monuments

Colorado National Monument contains canyons, dinosaur fossils, and remains of prehistoric Native American cultures; *Dinosaur National Monument* contains a quarry with dinosaur and other ancient animal fossils; *Florissant Fossil Beds National Monument* preserves the fossil remains of ancient insects as well as petrified trees; and *Hovenweep National Monument* is made up of six groups of cliff dwellings and pueblos built by Native Americans.

National Recreation Area

Curecanti National Recreation Area is made up of Blue Mesa, Crystal, and Morrow Point reservoirs, forming the largest body of water in Colorado.

National Forests

Colorado's national forests cover millions of acres of grassland and forest and include the *Rio Grande National Forest,* 1.86 million acres (753,000 ha) in southwestern Colorado.

State Parks

Colorado has 41 state parks. They include *Eldorado Canyon State Park,* which runs along scenic South Boulder Creek and provides excellent rock climbing opportunities for its visitors, and *State Forest State Park,* with its 71,000 acres (28,700 ha) of forest, jagged peaks, alpine lakes, wildlife, and miles of trails.

SPORTS TEAMS

NCAA Teams (Division I)

Colorado State University *Rams*
U.S. Air Force Academy *Falcons*
University of Colorado *Buffaloes*
University of Denver *Hawks*

PROFESSIONAL SPORTS TEAMS

Major League Baseball

Colorado *Rockies*

National Basketball Association

Denver *Nuggets*

National Football League

Denver *Broncos*

National Hockey League

Colorado *Avalanche*

Major League Soccer

Colorado *Rapids*

CULTURAL INSTITUTIONS

Libraries

Denver Public Library, the oldest library in the state, has one of the most extensive collections of Western history and genealogy in the nation, as well as a research center on African American history.

State Historical Society of Colorado (Denver) contains interesting historical documents on the early days of Colorado.

Museums

Colorado Springs Pioneers Museum (Colorado Springs) contains more than 40,000 objects that portray the history and culture of the Pikes Peak region. Includes an extensive regional art collection, Native American collection, and an archives and research library.

Boulder Museum of History chronicles the settlement and industrial development of Boulder. It is the steward of nearly 30,000 objects that convey the history of life in Boulder County from the 1800s to the present.

Colorado Historical Society (Denver) contains more than 125,000 artifacts and 8 million historical documents, including books, maps, photographs, diaries, and newspapers.

Denver Museum of Nature and Science (Denver) is the Rocky Mountain region's leading resource for informal science education.

Denver Art Museum (Denver), a work of art in its own right, houses 40,000 international artworks rotated in a variety of exhibits. It contains the most comprehensive body of objects from Africa in the Rocky Mountain region, including about 1,000 paintings, sculptures, and mixed-media compositions from every part of the continent.

Museum of Western Art (Denver) houses paintings and sculptures by a number of Western artists, including Frederic Remington, Charles M. Russell, and Thomas Moran.

Performing Arts

Colorado Ballet (Denver) has been performing for more than 50 years. Under the leadership of artistic director Gil Boggs, it has recently earned some of the best reviews of its history.

The *Colorado Symphony* (Denver) was established in 1989. It offers performances by a full-sized orchestra as well as smaller ensembles.

Universities and Colleges

In 2011, Colorado had 13 public and 39 private institutions of higher education.

ANNUAL EVENTS

January–March

National Western Stock Show in Denver (January)

Breckenridge Ullr Fest Winter Carnival (January)

Steamboat Springs Winter Carnival (February)

World Cup Ski Racing Competitions in Vail and Beaver Creek (February and March)

Durango Film Festival (March)

April–June

Taste of Vail (April)

Iron Horse Bicycle Classic in Durango (May)

Aspen Food & Wine Magazine Classic (June)

Glenwood Springs Strawberry Days (June)

Telluride Wine Festival (June)

Telluride Bluegrass Festival (June)

Frog Rodeo in Empire (June)

July–September

Denver Cherry Creek Arts Festival (July)

Central City Opera Festival (July and August)

Colorado Shakespeare Festival in Boulder (July and August)

Crested Butte Arts Festival in Crested Butte (August)

Colorado State Fair in Pueblo (August)

Larimer Square Oktoberfest in Denver (September)

October–December

Parade of Lights in Denver (December)

Electric Safari (Cheyenne Mountain Zoo) in Colorado Springs (December)

Copper Mountain resort

BIOGRAPHICAL DICTIONARY

Amy Adams (1974–), born in Italy, was raised in Castle Rock with her six siblings. After studying ballet and singing in her high school choir, Adams decided to pursue musical theater and film roles. She has starred in several popular films, including *Enchanted* and *Man of Steel*.

Eppie Archuleta (1922–) born in Santa Cruz, New Mexico, she is a sixth-generation blanket weaver who has made a contribution to the permanent art exhibit at the Smithsonian Institution.

India Arie (1975–) is a Grammy Award–winning R&B singer, songwriter, and record producer. Born in Denver to a former Motown singer and a professional basketball player, Arie has sold more than 10 million records worldwide.

Casimiro Barela (1847–1920), born in Embudo, New Mexico, insisted that the Colorado legislature print all laws in both English and Spanish and was one of the first people in the country to promote bilingual communication. He served in the Colorado legislature for more than 25 years.

James Beckwourth See page 44.

William Bent (1809–1869) and his brother established Bent's Fort, a trading post during Colorado's pioneer days. Born in St. Louis, Missouri, William Bent also served as a guide during the Mexican War (1846–48).

Jessica Biel (1982–) grew up in Boulder, where she studied dance and voice. Her career took off after she landed a role on the TV series *7th Heaven* at age 14. Biel is now a successful movie star.

Chauncey Billups (1976–), a five-time NBA All-Star, has played for several teams, including the Denver Nuggets. Billups attended George Washington High School in Denver and won two high school championships in basketball. After two years at the University of Colorado, he joined the NBA in 1997.

Charles Boettcher (1852–1948) came from his native Germany to Wyoming in 1869 and later moved to Denver. He built an empire based on selling whatever Coloradans needed—mining equipment, tools, household goods, sugar, and beef. He formed the Great Western Sugar Company with several friends, turning sugar beets into processed sugar.

Frederick Bonfils (1860–1933) moved to Denver in 1895 and, with a partner, bought and began publishing the *Denver Post* (formerly the *Evening Post*). He was born in Missouri.

Clara Brown (1800–1882), born in Virginia, began Denver's first Sunday school in 1859. Called the Angel of the Rockies, she operated a laundry for miners and offered housing for the homeless.

Margaret Brown (1867–1932), born in Hannibal, Missouri, was known as "Unsinkable Molly" Brown. She was a Denver socialite who survived the sinking of the *Titanic* in 1912.

Margaret Brown

M. Scott Carpenter

Ben Nighthorse Campbell See page 91.

M. Scott Carpenter (1925–2013) was one of the seven original Mercury astronauts. Born in Boulder, he flew the second American crewed orbital mission in 1962.

Ralph L. Carr (1887–1950), born in Rosita, served as governor of Colorado from 1939 to 1943. He is best remembered for opposing poor treatment of Japanese Americans during World War II.

Christopher "Kit" Carson See page 49.

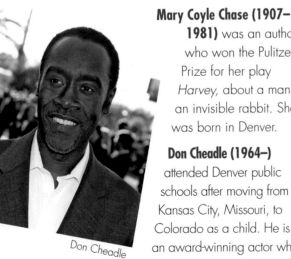

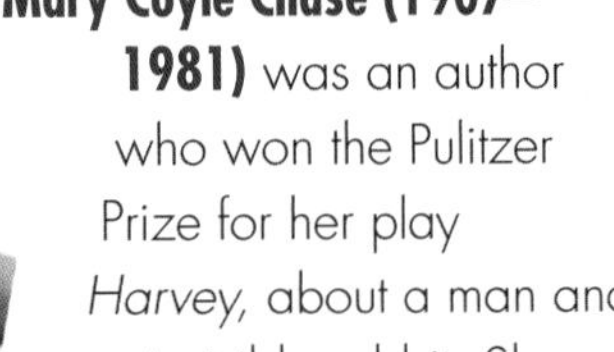

Mary Coyle Chase (1907–1981) was an author who won the Pulitzer Prize for her play *Harvey*, about a man and an invisible rabbit. She was born in Denver.

Don Cheadle

Don Cheadle (1964–) attended Denver public schools after moving from Kansas City, Missouri, to Colorado as a child. He is an award-winning actor who appeared in *Hamburger Hill*, *Hotel Rwanda*, and the *Iron Man* movies.

Chin Lin Sou (1836–1894), born in Doun Goon, China, went to Colorado during the gold rush. A miner and a railroad worker, he helped negotiate contracts between Chinese workers and business owners and ran a trading post that specialized in Chinese goods.

Chipeta (White Singing Bird) (1844–1924), born in the San Juan Mountains, was the second wife of Chief Ouray and a diplomat who helped negotiate peace between the Utes and the whites.

William "Buffalo Bill" Cody (1846–1917) was a guide, cavalryman, and showman from Scott County, Iowa. He brought the Wild West to eastern cities through his Wild West show and his stories that appeared in more than 400 dime novels.

Adolph Coors (1847–1929), founder of the Coors Brewery in Golden, began selling bottled beer, ale, and cider in 1873, and built his brewery into a major business venture. He was born in Barmen, Prussia.

Francisco Vásquez de Coronado See page 34.

Jack Dempsey (1895–1963), born in Manassa, was a heavyweight boxer. The "Manassa Mauler" held the world championship between 1919 and 1926.

John Denver (1943–1997), born Henry John Deutschendorf Jr., was a folk singer and songwriter known as a champion of the environment. "Rocky Mountain High" is one of his most well-known songs.

Father John Lewis Dyer (1812–1901) traveled the Rocky Mountains carrying the mail and preaching in the mining camps. Born in Minnesota, he was the first chaplain of Colorado's state senate.

John Elway (1960–), born in Port Angeles, Washington, played as quarterback for the Super Bowl–winning Denver Broncos. He is a member of the Pro Football Hall of Fame.

Elizabeth Piper Ensley (1848–1919) was born in the Caribbean Islands. She moved to Boston in the 1870s and, after getting married, headed west in the 1890s. She organized the Colorado Colored Women's Republican Club and worked to educate women about politics and voting.

Jose Raul Esquibel (1943–) uses his artistic skills to carve and create statues of saints, called santos. His santos appear in monasteries and churches throughout Colorado and New Mexico. He was born in Littleton.

Anne Evans (1871–1941) founded the Denver Artist's Club, which she helped evolve into the Denver Art Museum. Because she had an interest in Colorado's Native American heritage, the Denver Art Museum became one of the first museums to collect and exhibit Native American art.

Barney Ford See page 89.

Justina Warren Ford (1871–1952), born in Illinois, was Colorado's first African American female doctor. During her career, she delivered more than 7,000 babies, and provided medical care for all races, regardless of the patient's ability to pay.

Missy Franklin

Missy Franklin See page 79.

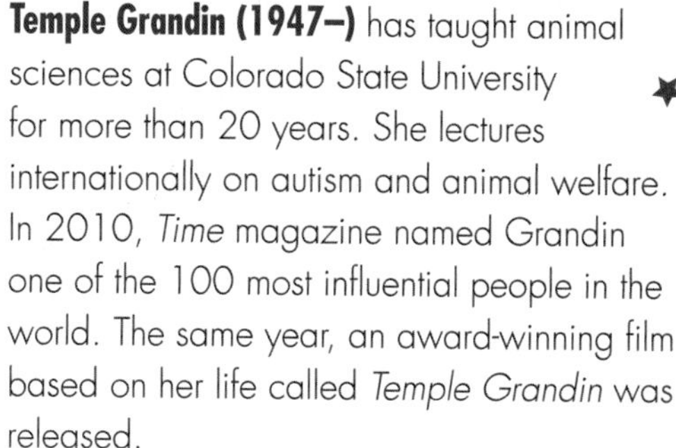

Temple Grandin (1947–) has taught animal sciences at Colorado State University for more than 20 years. She lectures internationally on autism and animal welfare. In 2010, *Time* magazine named Grandin one of the 100 most influential people in the world. The same year, an award-winning film based on her life called *Temple Grandin* was released.

Emily Griffith (1880–1947) founded the Emily Griffith Opportunity School, a national model for adult education, teaching English and job skills. She was born in Cincinnati, Ohio.

Ruth Mosko Handler (1938–2002), born in Denver, was a cofounder of the toymaker Mattel, Inc., and introduced the world to the Barbie doll in 1959. The company now sells more than 100 million Barbie dolls yearly.

Ruth Mosko Handler

Matt Hasselbeck (1975–), born in Boulder, is an NFL quarterback who started with the Green Bay Packers in 1999. He led the Seattle Seahawks to six playoff appearances and one Super Bowl appearance.

Linda Hogan See page 76.

Sadie Likens (1840–1920) moved to Denver from Trenton, Ohio, in the 1870s and became a leader in the Women's Christian Temperance Union. She cared for women and children, sick people, and war veterans.

Benjamin Barr Lindsey (1869–1943) helped establish Denver's first juvenile court and was strongly and vocally opposed to child labor. He was born in Tennessee.

Little Raven (?–1889) was an Arapaho chief who is remembered for welcoming the white settlers to the Denver area. He lived in a decorated tepee and invited whites to talk and share meals. He was camped at Sand Creek when the massacre occurred in 1864. He survived, but he and other Arapahos never trusted the U.S. government again.

Hattie McDaniel (1895–1952) moved from Wichita, Kansas, to Colorado as a child. She became famous as an actress. She was the first African American to win an Academy Award, which she received for her role in *Gone with the Wind*.

Rachel B. Noel (1918–2008) was an educator and politician in Denver. Her work helped lead to the end of segregation in Denver's public schools.

Chief Ouray See page 51.

Owl Woman (1800?–1847) was the wife of William Bent, a Colorado pioneer and trader. Born in southwestern Colorado, she worked at Bent's Fort and often took charge of the supply trains.

Chief Ouray

William Jackson Palmer (1836–1909), born in Delaware, achieved great success and wealth in the railroad industry in Colorado. He founded Colorado Springs in 1871 and gave land and funds to several schools in the area.

Federico Peña

Federico Peña (1947–) took a job in Denver in 1973 as a lawyer for the Mexican American Legal Defense Fund. In 1983, he became the first Hispanic mayor of Denver. Peña was named the U.S. secretary of transportation in 1993 and the U.S. secretary of energy in 1997.

Spencer Penrose (1865–1939) invested in various mining and real estate projects in Colorado, making a fortune in the gold mining industry. Born in Philadelphia, he supported many Colorado institutions, including the Colorado Springs Fine Arts Center, Pikes Peak Highway, and the Fountain Valley School.

Antoinette Perry (1888–1946) was an actress, manager, and producer. The Tony awards for Broadway plays are named in her honor. She was born in Denver.

Zebulon Pike See page 12.

Monica Pleiman (1964–) is chief executive officer and chairman of the board of directors of Optimum Management Systems, a business consulting firm. She traces her Colorado roots back 200 years to Spanish settlers. She won the Latina Entrepreneur Award in 2006.

Condoleezza Rice (1954–), born in Birmingham, Alabama, entered the University of Denver at age 15 and earned a doctorate in international studies there. Later, President George W. Bush named her national security adviser and then secretary of state. Rice was the first African American woman to hold either position.

AnnaSophia Robb (1993–) began acting professionally at age 11. She has starred in the films *Because of Winn-Dixie*, *Charlie and the Chocolate Factory*, and *Soul Surfer*. She was born in Denver.

Josephine Roche (1886–1976), born in Nebraska, was Denver's first policewoman. She was an activist who worked to help women and miners.

Florence Sabin See page 61.

Ken Salazar (1955–) served as attorney general for Colorado, U.S. senator for the state, and secretary of the interior in the Obama administration from 2009 to 2013. He was born in Alamosa.

Maria Teresa Sandoval (1811–1894) cofounded a trading post at Fort El Pueblo, where furs and hides were bought from trappers and traded for goods. She was born in Taos, New Mexico.

Hazel Schmoll See page 19.

Robert W. Speer (1855–1918) was Denver's mayor (1904–1912 and 1916–1918) and is often credited with beautifying the city. He was born in Pennsylvania.

Horace Tabor (1830–1899) was a prospector, merchant, and politician. He made a fortune in silver mining—and lost it after the crash in 1893—and served as the first mayor of Leadville. He was born in Vermont.

Amy Van Dyken

Amy Van Dyken (1973–) is an Olympic gold medalist in swimming. She took up the sport to overcome her problems with asthma. She was born in Englewood.

Wellington Webb (1941–), born in Chicago, was Denver's first African American mayor, serving from 1991 to 2003.

Byron R. White (1917–2002), born in Fort Collins, served on the U.S. Supreme Court from 1962 to 1993. Byron "Whizzer" White is the only justice to have played college and professional football—and been a member of the Football Hall of Fame! Appointed by President John F. Kennedy, White was considered a moderate justice. He died at the age of 84 in Denver.

Byron R. White

Paul Whiteman (1890–1967) trained in classical music but became a popular jazz musician and orchestra leader. Born in Denver, he became known as the King of Jazz in the 1920s.

YieMei See page 74.

RESOURCES

BOOKS

Nonfiction

Becker, Cynthia S. *Chipeta: Ute Peacemaker*. Palmer Lake, Colo.: Filter Press, 2008.

Collier, Grant. *Colorado's National Parks & Monuments*. Lakewood, Colo.: Collier, 2010.

Getz, Charmaine Ortega. *Weird Colorado: Your Travel Guide to Colorado's Local Legends and Best Kept Secrets*. New York: Sterling, 2010.

Lohse, Joyce B. *General William Palmer: Railroad Pioneer*. Palmer Lake, Colo.: Filter Press, 2009.

Saccomano, Jim. *Denver Broncos: The Complete Illustrated History*. Minneapolis, Minn.: MBI, 2013.

Turner, Carol. *Forgotten Heroes and Villains of Sand Creek*. Charleston, S.C.: History Press, 2010.

Fiction

Carbone, Elisa. *Last Dance on Holladay Street*. New York: Laurel Leaf, 2006.

Creel, Ann Howard. *Water at the Blue Earth*. Lanham, Md.: Roberts Rinehart Publishers, 1998.

Eagle-Walking Turtle. *Full Moon Stories*. New York: Hyperion, 1997.

Hobbs, Will. *Beardance*. New York: Aladdin, 2004.

James, Will. *Cowboy in the Making*. Missoula, Mont.: Mountain Press, 2001.

Lawlor, Laurie. *Crossing the Colorado Rockies, 1864*. New York: Aladdin, 2001.

FACTS FOR NOW

Visit this Scholastic Web site for more information on Colorado:
www.factsfornow.scholastic.com
Enter the keyword **Colorado**

INDEX

★ ★ ★

Page numbers in *italics* indicate illustrations.

AUTHOR'S TIPS AND SOURCE NOTES

★ ★ ★

Research for this book required extensive trips to the library, a tour through www.amazon.com, and endless hours searching the Internet. For some useful sites about Colorado, you can visit www.factsfornow.scholastic.com and enter the keyword **Colorado**.

The best book I used as a reference was *A Colorado History* by Carl Ubbelohde, Maxine Benson, and Duane A. Smith. Another fine reference is *Colorado: A History of the Centennial State* by Carol Abbott. Other print works that proved invaluable in the writing of this book were *Colorado, Yesterday & Today* by Grant Collier and Joseph Collier, and *Colorado 1870–2000 Revisited* and *The Colorado Almanac: Facts about Colorado*, both by Thomas J. Noel.

Photos ©: age footstock/Chase Jarvis: 14; Alamy Images: 5 top right, 56 bottom (Daniel Templeton), 4 bottom left, 74 top (David Muenker), 115 right (David W. Hamilton), 103 (Jim West), 19 right (Robert E. Barber), 96 (Ryan McGinnis), 113 top (Stephen Saks Photography), 19 left (Tom Uhlman); AP Images: 87, 92 inset (Brennan Linsley), 85 (Craig F. Walker, The Denver Post), 136 right (Joe Marquette); Art Resources: 49 (Bill Manns), 37, 122 (Culver Pictures), 24 top, 25 left (Scala/Museum of the City of New York); Aspen Colors Studio: 74 bottom; Boulder County Farmers' Market: 112 right; Centennial Museum/The University of Texas at El Paso: 4 top center, 25 bottom right, 31; Colorado Historical Society: 48 (Decorative and Fine Arts Department, CHS-X20087), 89 (F6323); Corbis Images: 44, 57 top, 58, 61, 134 top, 37 bottom (Bettmann); 76 top (Christopher Felver), 108 top (George H. H. Huey), 78 (Larry W. Smith/epa), 32 bottom, 34 right, 34 left detail (Norman Price/Bettmann), 102 (Steve Starr), 121 (Tim OLeary/zefa), 111 bottom (Tom Bean), 4 top left, 22, 108 bottom, 120 (W. Perry Conway), 12, 33 bottom, 118; Dembinsky Photo Associates/John Pennoyer: 113 bottom; Denver Public Library, Western History Collection: 42 top, 43 left (D. H. Huyept, Z-4046), 133 (Denver Post, X-21713), 41 (John R. Henderson, Z-3073), 51, 136 left (Noah H. Rose, X-30713), 43 top, 45 (Otto Westerman, X-981), 57 bottom, 60 (Tom Parker, X-6560), 50 (X-11858), 5 top left, 42 bottom, 46 (X-60186), 54 (Z-8811); Getty Images: 137 top (Al Bello), 71 (Hyoung Chang/The Denver Post), 79 inset, 135 left (Javier Soriano/AFP), 65 (Joe Amon/The Denver Post), 63 (Karl Gehring/The Denver), 134 bottom (Kevin Winter), 91 (MPI), 80, 81 left (PhotoLink), 16 (Scott Warren), 97 top, 99, 4 bottom right (Tyler Stableford); Inmagine: 81 top, 94, 126 bottom; iStockphoto: back cover (Adventure_Photo), 130 top (David Freund), 116 bottom, 130 bottom (Geoffrey Black), 43 bottom, 123 (Hannamaria Photography), 8, 9 left (Missing35mm), 128 (Vladislav Lebedinski), 116 top left, 117; Lonely Planet Images/Richard Cummins: 64; Media Bakery: cover; Minden Pictures: 25 bottom left, 28 (Wil Meinderts/Foto Natura), 114 bottom (Yva Momatiuk/John Eastcott); National Geographic Stock/Roy Andersen: 25 top, 26; Nativestock.com/Marilyn "Angel" Wynn: 24 bottom, 29; North Wind Picture Archives: 4 top right, 33 top, 38; Omni-Photo Communications/W. Lynn Seldon Jr.: 105, 132; Patricia Switzer: 67 top, 76 bottom; Peter Arnold Inc.: 124 (Hannamaria Photography), 5 bottom, 109 (Jeff Greenberg); PhotoEdit/Michelle D. Bridwell: 110 right; Reuters: 90 (Ed Andrieski), 135 right (Jeff Christensen); Robertstock.com/Michael DeYoung: 23; Science Source: 10 (James Steinberg), 115 left (Kenneth Murray); StockFood: 73 (Paul Poplis Photography, Inc.), 72 (Maximilian Stock - StockFood Munich); Superstock, Inc.: cover inset (Cusp), 66 (Jim West/age fotostock), 79 left, 127 (Ron Dahlquist), 9 top, 21, 98 (Stock Connection); The Granger Collection: 32, 33 left, 56 top, 57 left; The Image Works: 114 top (Hermann Dornhege/VISUM), 82, 110 left (Rob Crandall), 104 (Sean Cayton); University of Colorado/Casey Cass: 112 left; US Mint: 111 top, 111 center, 116 top right, 119; Vector-Images.com: 95, 126 top.

Maps by Map Hero, Inc.